ENDORSEMENTS

In this book, Ashley describes how we as Christians are in a daily battle, living in a world that is trying to dictate how we think, speak and act. As I read this book, it really convicted me; I could identify with Ashley in the revelations given to her from the Lord: how we can fall into the trap of mindless circumstances that compete with having our Savior as the true priority. I love how Ashley shows a true contrast in worldly confusion experienced in daily living, and how she presents the reality of how we are to combat those mindsets with the commands and words of the living God. This book challenges us as Christians to seek an authentic life; to be set apart!

Do we make the time for God? Ashley pushes us to see how this commitment to God can change our lives. In a world where everywhere we turn, we are influenced on what to think, what to believe, how to act, what we should and shouldn't do, we have lost sight of God and how He is truly the antidote to all of our struggles. Ashley establishes the various road blocks we have in our relationship with God. She helps us to navigate through life experiences by means of scripture. Be prepared to learn about yourself as Ashley demonstrates and proves how these daily distractions prevent us from a true relationship with God that will forever change you.

In *Authentic*, Ashley removes a mask that is dominant in our society today in a way that I hope encourages you to let who you were created to be from the foundations of the earth become the very essence of who you are. It's a call back to the unique, customized plan of God, sealed in you that can't be taken away, altered or destroyed. It's whose voice we listen to that creates the next scenario, decision, emotion etc. He wants to display His glory through you. Will you accept His invitation?

Authentic: Taking off the Mask of the World —Copyright ©2023 by Ashley Babicka

Published by UNITED HOUSE Publishing
All rights reserved. No portion of this book may be reproduced or shared in any form–electronic, printed, photocopied, recording, or by any information storage and retrieval system, without prior written permission from the publisher. The use of short quotations is permitted.

ISBN: 978-1-952840-38-8

UNITED HOUSE Publishing
Waterford, Michigan
info@unitedhousepublishing.com
www.unitedhousepublishing.com

All Scripture quotations, unless otherwise indicated, are taken from the Holy Bible, New International Version®, NIV®. Copyright ©1973, 1978, 1984, 2011 by Biblica, Inc.™ Used by permission of Zondervan. All rights reserved worldwide. www.zondervan.comThe "NIV" and "New International Version" are trademarks registered in the United States Patent and Trademark Office by Biblica, Inc.™

Cover layout and interior design:
Talitha McGuinness, talitha@unitedhousepublishing.com
Printed in the United States of America

2023—First Edition
SPECIAL SALES
Most UNITED HOUSE books are available at special quantity discounts when purchased in bulk by corporations, organizations, and special-interest groups. For information, please e-mail orders@unitedhousepublishing.com.

DEDICATION

To those who are tired of what the world has told you and want to live a better way. God's way.

ACKNOWLEDGMENTS

To my best friend, thank you for trusting me to write this. To my husband, thank you for always being a support and light, on days I felt alone. To my children, thank you for allowing me to be your mom.

AUTHENTIC
TAKING **OFF** THE MASK OF THE **WORLD**

BECOMING
WHO
GOD'S
CALLED
YOU
TO
BE

ASHLEY BABICKA

CONTENTS

Endorsements 1
Copyright 2
Dedication 3
Acknowledgments 5

INTRO 11

PART ONE: MASKS OF THE WORLD 15
    Mask One: Over-Scheduled 17
    Mask Two: Pressure to Prove 27

PART TWO: GOD'S AUTHENTIC PLAN 35
    God's Authentic Plan: The Gospel 37
    God's Authentic Plan: Rest 47
    God's Authentic Plan: Prayer 55
    God's Authentic Plan: Engaging with the Father 63

PART THREE: LIVING AUTHENTICALLY WILL REQUIRE 75
    Living Authentically Will Require: Knowing What to Take Off and What to Put On 77
    Living Authentically Will Require: Continual Choice 85
    Living Authentically Will Require: New Goals 91
    Living Authentically Will Require: An Acceptance of the Mantle 101
    Living Authentically Will Require: Acknowledging that the Plans Have Changed 111
    Living Authentically Will Require: Bravery 119

CONCLUSION 131
BIBLIOGRAPHY 132

AUTHENTIC

INTRO

I want to pose a question to you. Do you think you are wearing a mask? Do you feel that you are living authentically? Is there anything you can identify in your life right now that is causing you to conceal your relationship with God? Or is there anything causing you to disguise who God made you to be?

Our world operates with many masks, trying to cover up and conceal who God is and what He's called us to do. Growing up, I loved waiting in line at the grocery store. It was a place my parents probably disliked. Each time we stood there waiting as the cashier rang up the groceries, I would beg for candy. Well, maybe not every time, but I sure did ask a lot. There were so many good sweet treats. After a number of no's, I'd stare at the only other thing in the checkout lines. I know you're probably thinking there are toys, gift cards, and Chapstick. Yes, I know, but I want you to remember the early 1990s. There wasn't anything other than candy and magazines that littered the aisle.

I would scan the magazines and pick up one with all the latest details about *NSYNC and The Backstreet Boys. As I flipped through the soft pages, I began to understand something I would struggle to shake, even into my thirties: that the world had an ideal. There was a physical look, body shape, and pants size I should have as a woman. My hair should look a particular way, and of course, clothes and name brands were key. As a teenager, I not only began to see what the world's standards were, but also how far off I was from them.

So began a decade-plus journey of trying to emulate what I thought I should be. This didn't just manifest in physical terms but also in how I spent money, lived my life, and justified my behaviors. It was exhausting. Of course, I didn't know it then, it was just normal. But now looking back, I realize things were so off. Even after believing Jesus was my Lord and Savior and getting involved in church, I found myself still very bound by the world's standards. The sweet craving for what was familiar had me back in line time and time again.

One of the things I learned later in my life is that God calls us to live apart from the world. He has an authentic plan for our lives. God desires for us to live in a complete relationship with Him, free from the many things that oppress us or steal our focus. Much like our ancestors Adam and Eve, we find ourselves hiding behind things in our world. But God never intended for us to hide. Yes, I know the world says it's normal, but it's not God's authentic plan.

In my early 30s, I found myself worn out and tired of the things that were considered normal, and I began a journey with God to find out what it means to live authentically. I began to sit with Him and search His Word for clarity on how to live bravely and with confidence. And in that process, He began to reveal to me the need to address sin in my life I had not yet recognized and what He desired to see in my character as a Christ follower. The lens began to shift from the world's views to Biblical truth. I wanted to learn what it felt like to live free.

In the process, I found the greatest reward to be closeness to the Father. If you don't know who the Father is, my prayer is you will by the time you finish reading through these pages. My prayer is you will see the love story He left for you in His Word and the way He intimately and personally made you. He has created you to live a life of authenticity and freedom. This world might say it offers the same, but any imitation item is not equal.

I pray you can take a moment to see how much freedom you actually have, to take off that superficial mask you've been putting on, and see that what you've been experiencing and going through isn't abnormal but actually quite typical. I pray you would not only be able to see how much God loves you but also see how much the enemy tries to distort what God's intentions are for you. I pray you would be able to learn to love yourself, the parts you feel ashamed about, the parts that don't make sense, the parts others say aren't enough. Well, they are enough, my friend. You are enough. These aren't just words I'm typing and putting on paper to make you feel inspired. They are true words; words I've come to believe about myself. And I want so badly for you to believe it, too.

Feeling like we are enough all hinges on our ability to not only believe God's Word but also be transformed by it. Romans 12:2, NIV says,

Do not conform to the pattern of this world, but be transformed by the renewing of your mind. Then you will be able to test and approve what God's will is—his good, pleasing and perfect will.

We will never be able to live authentic, God-centered lives if we don't get in the habit of renewing our minds and focusing on things from God's perspective. Stop feeling like you have to hide your real self to present a more polished or perfect version of yourself to others. That was never God's authentic plan. Come out of the shadows. He's got freedom waiting for you, and it's so much sweeter than a piece of candy.

AUTHENTIC

PART ONE: MASKS OF THE WORLD

Learning to live authentically, starts with us removing the masks we've been putting on. Mask is defined as: Something that serves to conceal or disguise.[1]

AUTHENTIC

MASK ONE:
Over-Scheduled

My husband has to regularly remind me to share my Google calendar with him. I often put things on my calendar but fail to inform him of what's coming up. Well, actually, I do, but it's often just days before an event or dinner I've already confirmed with someone else. I find my calendar has the potential to simply get away from me. A busy calendar can be a potential disguise for not being obedient or available to hear from God.

I think Satan desires for us to find our schedules so busy that we struggle to find time with God in His Word, let alone to pray or be patient to hear his voice. But what do you do when the world screams, "You don't want to miss that," or when your inner self says, "You'll be able to rest next week," or "This is normal"? We have become great at being able to encourage poor behaviors and patterns and less successful at being able to call out what doesn't align with a life of presence.

When I say the word "presence," what comes to mind? For me, I think of my daughter. I think of how much has changed in her first year of life, and it felt like, even though I was home with her, I was unable to capture all the moments and remember all the things she was doing. It is a weird feeling to know that you have stopped to be present, yet you still feel distracted, unable to grasp the moments.

I believe our presence is of great value to God. I think about how gentle and sweet He is when I'm in His presence. How He lavishes me with love and holds me close. I think about how His

Word comes to life as I read the Bible, and He reveals things to me that my human mind can't fathom. I think of His subtle, not forceful, nature. His presence is something that I desire to experience. But just because I want to be present with my child, God, husband, family, and friends, doesn't mean that I will be.

Presence requires stillness. It requires a turning off of other things to focus on one thing. It requires a heart that's not distracted or disturbed. Above all else, it requires time. If our schedules are jam packed with work, after school activities, sports, events with friends, and church activities, we find ourselves grasping for mere minutes with God, instead of hours.

What does your calendar currently look like? Is it jam-packed to the point where if God asked you to do something, there's no room for Him? Is your schedule packed so full you don't have to deal with the issues that the Lord keeps bringing up to you? Is your schedule full because you lack the courage to say "no"? May I propose that by not saying "no" to them, you're saying "no" to you or "no" to God? There is always a "no"; it's just a matter of which area of our lives we place it.

Saying "yes" to putting in the extra hours at work could look like saying "no" to family time or time in the Word. Saying "yes" to a friend who is clearly toxic for you could mean you are saying "no" to the relationship God actually called you to with a core friend. Saying "yes" to trips could look like saying "no" to making space for the sabbath and rest with God. Saying "yes" to doing more at church when you're already stretched thin, could be saying "no" to your peace. With every "yes," there's a "no."

There is a tendency to believe that giving of oneself is what should be done in all settings. We can, at times, overestimate our own value, believing that if we don't step in or fill the gap, it will remain open. This is important to bring up because part of overscheduled lives lies in the balance of overcommitting and trying to fill voids that God can fill better.

In the process, we end up becoming distracted from what matters most, end up feeling exhausted from our endeavors, and eventually find ourselves enslaved to a pattern that doesn't mimic the desires of our Father. These three things: distraction, exhaustion, and enslavement all play a role in masking who God is to us and others.

I'd love for us to look at each area and for you to really be honest with yourself and where you could be at. For some distraction could be playing a bigger role than exhaustion. And for others, you may feel enslaved and like freedom seems impossible. I want to encourage you before we ever jump into these areas, that taking off a mask and living a healthier, God centered life is not easy, not many choose that path. It will cause us to at times have to look at dysfunction that we've accepted as normal and ask ourselves, "am I going to change behaviors to fix this?"

I'm so grateful for Jesus and the fact that with him nothing is impossible. Overcoming a busy life is not impossible. God will and can show us the way to His freedom, if we are willing to allow Him to do the heart work on us. Our busyness is a heart issue and whether we like it or not, our heart has found gratification in distraction.

Living Overscheduled Leads to Distraction

In my human nature, there are times when I approach God, expecting to encounter His presence to hear from Him, yet my heart and mind are distracted. Distraction is, unfortunately, a part of life. I just think too many of us excuse distractions and overscheduled lives as normal. I want to paint the picture that distraction is significant and can not only waste valuable time for the Kingdom of God, but it is also one of the primary tools of Satan.

Distraction in our schedules could look like travel sports for our kids, multiple church events in a week, being consumed with cleaning your house or tidying up outside for appearances, working late, watching hours of television at night, and meetings with people. They don't present themselves as distractions on the surface, they appear to be opportunities. But any of the things listed above are distractions if they are causing us to drift away from God. Drifting away from God isn't just a reading-your-Bible thing, it's a marriage thing, it's a family thing, it's a time thing.

We can at times have a very narrow view of what it looks like to be distracted. And in a world that celebrates being able to multitask, it can often be seen as unwise to remain focused on one thing with intention. One of the verses I find so sad in scripture is Judges 16:20, NIV,

Then she called, 'Samson, the Philistines are upon you!' He awoke from his sleep and thought, 'I'll go out as before and shake myself free.' But he did not know that the Lord had left him.

The Lord left Samson. How I hope that day never happens for you or me. Samson's distraction is what led him to this point. He was distracted by lust. His lust gave him over to the Philistines. He likely didn't see Delilah as a distraction, much like things in our lives. And before you know it, he forgot about and forsook the Lord.

He forgot about the One who had helped him kill a lion and many Philistines before; the One who comforted him after the death of his wife. It wasn't intentional, but it happened. Satan is a master at distraction, and Satan wants you to live a life where you only experience a fraction of what God has for you. Satan will use people, things, shopping, family, work, entertainment, hobbies, and the church as distractions.

Our world has tried to program us to consume, consume, consume, manifesting in us short attention spans and difficulty remaining still. We are easily distracted but struggle to remain. On the surface, distraction and busyness present themselves as productivity, but in the end only lead us further from our Lord.

Living overscheduled lives doesn't just lead to distraction, but it tends to eventually cause us to pick up the baton of exhaustion too. These two go hand in hand, while we are distracted we are unaware of the reality that this is not possible to maintain long term. So we continue to say 'yes' to things while we are distracted and before we know it wish we hadn't. Exhaustion begins to set in and we are left feeling absolutely depleted.

Living Overscheduled Leads to Exhaustion

What's exhausting you about your busy calendar? When I think of exhaustion I see it as the body's physical response to the hardship or trauma we are putting it through. As a parent, there have been many sleepless nights where I felt exhausted the next morning. The exhaustion came from a lack of sleep. If there's an area in which you are feeling exhausted, it is representative of an area of lack in your life.

We have become great at stuffing our bodies with things to help compensate for the exhaustion, instead of filling ourselves with God. Not sure if I have any coffee drinkers reading, but at times I've used this as a crutch to mask the actual issue—I was too busy and needed to remove something from my calendar. I needed to sit with my Father. So instead of getting to the root issue, I merely skimmed the top of the iceberg with a couple extra cups of coffee a day. But true transformation doesn't happen if we don't get down to the heart of what's driving our decision making.

The root problem with living a continual lifestyle of busyness can lie in one of two areas: a legalistic mindset or an inability to accept grace. Legalism isn't just something applied to faith or religion but is a way we can view and experience our day-to-day life as well. Legalism says this is what you have to do, and there's no room for error or edits. It's based on a fear mindset that something could be screwed up or some moral code may be broken. The way we see life can often be very legalistic, sometimes operating more out of fear than freedom.

Coupled with that legalism there can be an inability to give oneself grace; grace to not get it all right today or tomorrow, grace to rest if needed, grace to say "no" and know I'm still a great friend, and grace to put down the list of "to-do's" and allow God to define the day. The root problem with exhaustion comes down to thinking. Do you find yourself falling into one of these two categories with your calendar—accepting things from a place of legalism or lack of grace for your current needs?

Exhaustion is a part of this world's DNA. It's unavoidable, we're told, but I've never been a person who likes being told that I 'have to' accept something. I want to know why. And I want the freedom to choose it for myself. Exhaustion is a choice. I'm not sure if anyone has told you that before.

Your calendar is a good indicator of the exhaustion you will naturally be led to, or not, in your week. Both what is on your calendar and how full it is are determining factors. Our bodies were not created to be houses of exhaustion. That was never a part of God's authentic plan. Quite the opposite, actually—we were created for relationship and union with the Father, to experience peace and joy. But when we make decisions about things on our calendars that are rooted in legalism or a lack of grace for ourselves, we are sure to push ourselves to the boundary lines of exhaustion.

I've met people and know people who do this repeatedly. I used to do it myself. They coin the saying, "It's just a busy season" but rarely do they ever have their heads above water. The repetition of the busy calendar, their distraction from what's getting off course, and overall exhaustion physically, end up causing what I see as enslavement. I've been like a fish on a rod, feeling as though I no longer had the ability to guide where my body, time, or energies were going. Before you know it the mind, body, and heart adapt to chaos and busyness as mere everyday life.

Usually people who are walking through this struggle never intended to feel this way. It was merely a series of decisions over a prolonged time that led them to this place. I want to encourage you to be very aware of your choices, because all choices lead to life or death. To freedom or enslavement.

Living Overscheduled Leads to Enslavement

The definition of enslavement is: to reduce to slavery or to SUBJUGATE.[2] Enslavement's intent is to make one submissive or to control someone. One of the most common places of control in our world today is money. People make many money decisions with their calendars. Whether it's to fund a new car, lip injections, shopping, eating out, drinking, name brand bags, Sephora, travel, or buying things for our home, money is often driving our calendars. We have been programmed to believe that more is better and it bleeds into our schedules and lives.

If you were to look at your calendar, how much of it is filled with work? Do you spend extra hours, outside of 9am-5pm, working regularly? Is bringing work home a normal part of your week? Does your work consume more of your time at home than your family? I'm not saying work in and of itself is bad. God calls us to work and to be purposeful in it, to work with integrity and character. But when we are making decisions with our time that center on acquiring more of anything, including money, it can lead to a slippery slope.

> *No one can serve two masters. Either you will hate the one and love the other, or you will be devoted to the one and despise the other. You cannot serve both God and money.*
> Matthew 6:24, NIV

We can't serve money and God at the same level; there's a choice we have to make. The trap is that the need for money and making more of it requires more effort at work. With ever increasing demands in the workplace it can become easy to find ourselves throwing in extra hours, meetings, and ultimately energy to try and meet the demands of the job. This isn't a bad thing every now and again, but if it becomes a normal part of your weeks and months, it could be pointing to a bigger issue.

What is interesting to me is that nowhere in the Bible does it say that money is something that gives purpose, passion, joy, or peace. God never says that if one attains a great deal of money, one will attain health or success. Yet, we treat money like it's the end all, be all. How many decisions on your calendar are related to, or impacted by money? Do you feel freedom to say 'no' at your job? Do you think it's okay to stop work after a certain hour?

I wonder if some of us have lost the reverence and gratitude that God has supplied us with our jobs and ultimately is the one worthy of our time and attention first; that God has given us our families not to support first, but to love and train up in the way they should go. It's easy to lack boundaries in this world, it's becoming increasingly normal. I love that Jesus says,

*Come to me, all you who are weary and burdened,
and I will give you rest.*
Matthew 11:28, NIV

Christ's rest looks far different from the world's idea of rest; part of the rest he offers will require us to lay down our spirit of mammon. We can no longer desire worldly things, money, and activities more than God. Our time with God must come first, and our time with our spouse and children must come second. Picking up his yoke means laying down yours. And the beautiful thing is if we lay down the yoke of enslavement, we will also be laying down distraction and exhaustion. No longer will we be chasing people or their opinions. Even our own perceptions of ourselves and worth will change.

The mask of living over scheduled is not God's best for you, it's not His authentic plan. He is not blessed by your attempts to attain more by working harder or lacking appropriate boundaries. He's not asking you to carry more so he can push you to complete exhaustion. God is watching you and I, saddened that we feel we need to prove our worth when Jesus already proved everything needed on the cross. I imagine God wondering why we choose bondage over freedom. Living a life of busyness is not a mask you have to put on any longer. Living distracted, exhausted, and enslaved is not something you have to continue to say 'yes' to. There is a better way, friend. But before we get there, we need to take a look at one more mask that may be hindering you.

AUTHENTIC

MASK TWO:
Pressure to Prove

The first house my husband and I bought had a gravel driveway. After living in our home for a little over two years, the gravel was pretty worn out and in need of a fresh dump. So I was certain once we got a little extra money, we would, in fact, fix the driveway. We worked on cleaning up the front yard, planting plants, laying down new mulch, weed eating, and laying new grass seed. Our curb appeal was off to a great start. Now it was time for the driveway.

As I planned for the driveway installation, I called around and received quotes from various companies, which was totally logical. I only ran into one small problem: God saying, "No." It wasn't like a "No, you can never re-gravel your driveway," but more like, "No, not now." While I pitched a fit, internally kicking and screaming like a kid at the store after they're told they can't have candy in the checkout line, I felt so clearly God said no because I was doing it for the wrong reasons.

Now, I know I told you our driveway was really bad. That was true. But a huge driving force was our neighbors. Their yard and driveway were so well maintained. You may have that neighbor with a pristine yard, always mowing once a week and leaving lines in their grass. Those neighbors are great because they care, but it's also the worst because, even in your best attempt to care, you still sometimes feel like your yard is, well, just okay.

We were in a hurry to fix our driveway partially because I felt they looked at our driveway as an eyesore. It's as though I thought they woke up and looked out their office window each day and said, "Wow, those Babickas! When are they going to clean up that driveway, or better yet, get cement? Don't they see that it's ugly and those weeds are coming through? They must not care as we do." This dialogue was all going on in my head, which was really the driving force of the driveway refacing emergency.

God has to have a sense of humor because, within a week, two neighbors got truckloads of gravel dropped off, including the neighbor across the street! I mean, come on. But, as I laugh even thinking about this, I also smile because the pressure to prove didn't win that time. God's Word did.

While I waited for God to say "Yes," he was doing work on my heart. God was showing me that my driveway looking new and neat for the neighbors was not only an impossible way to live, but it was also inauthentic. God didn't create me to prove my value or worth to others, but to love and worship him alone.

Feeling the pressure to prove or perform distracts from living authentically. Something that is authentic is made or done the same way as an original.[3] Therefore, living "authentically" means living as God intended us to live—in His image. Are there areas in your life where you feel you aren't living as God has asked you to? Are there things that you're engaging in that are not an accurate reflection of your character, but you're doing it to fit in?

This feeling of pressure to prove oneself can be found in dating relationships, finances, appearances, our churches, parenting, and Christmas (which is truly ridiculous to be stressed about giving enough. Been there, done that). And while I just scratched the surface, dare I say that pressure and proving oneself never led to a person being authentic. Instead, it places more expectations on a person to live in conflict with their original design. Eventually this pressure to prove leads to stress and fear in our lives, feeling as though you "have to" do things for people, and ultimately sin.

These three things: stress and fear, feeling we 'have to,' and sin are all byproducts of feeling the pressure to prove to people. While we have been brought up in a culture that tells us we need to assimilate since birth, I want to encourage you while you read along to allow yourself to get a bit uncomfortable. To see yourself as an individual, not one in a room of many. To allow yourself to feel the weight that people pleasing is actually having on you spiritually, physically, and emotionally. I know trying to run from feelings is easier, it feels better. But I'm believing that leaning in will result in revelation. Before you move on to these parts, I'd encourage you to pray and allow the Lord to reveal what He wants to in these areas.

Living With the Pressure to Prove Leads to Stress and Fear

I know for myself, one of the areas I've continually struggled with stress and fear is in the area of proving my worth to others. For many years I was unaware of the decisions I was making to try and seek people's approval. Decisions like taking on more at work, trying to present a perfectly clean home, trying to look like the perfect Christian, trying to be the best friend, or trying to act like everything was okay in life. This vail of proving to people that Ashley was doing good was driving underlying tension.

When it comes to pressure to prove, I notice that stress and fear come into play because my priorities are out of order. I have been made to seek God's approval. God is seated above all of mankind. So my very seeking of affirmation from His created people is like trying to seek praise from a tree. It was created to help bring life to me, but it's not intended to be something I'm feeling pressure to perform for.

If we're not careful, we can find ourselves more focused on receiving approval from people, that we don't look for it from God. Often my issue with people pleasing is rooted in control. I want to control how they view me or the opportunities I'm given. I know that word is something that the world celebrates. People want to be in control of their finances, careers, children, and 401Ks. We want to live authentic lives that line up with God's Word. Nowhere in God's Word do I read that we are to be in control; in fact, repeatedly, He tells us to trust Him.

Take delight in the Lord, and he will give you the desires of your heart. Commit your way to the Lord; trust in him and he will do this.
Psalm 37:4-5, NIV

Trust in the Lord with all your heart and lean not on your own understanding; in all your ways submit to him, and he will make your paths straight.
Proverbs 3:5-6, NIV

For I know the plans I have for you, declares the Lord, plans to prosper you and not to harm you, plans to give you hope and a future.
Jeremiah 29:11, NIV

When I'm trying to control outcomes and situations, I've willingly invited stress and fear into the picture. Because the outcome being favorable depends on my ability, not God's. I've tried to step into His position.

There are times when I've thrown a party and found myself making decisions out of a place of fear because of what I perceived people would say. There are times when I've put pressure on myself to look or perform perfectly at my job, so I felt stressed about living up to those standards over and over again. There are times I've told myself there were certain things I had to "do" to be a good Christian and allowed fear of man to creep in when I thought I wasn't living up to those standards. I don't know what it may be for you, but I imagine there are a few ways you're currently stressing yourself out because you are placing pressure on yourself to prove something.

Are there areas in your life that you can identify as pressure points? Where do you feel you are making a decision out of proving value or establishing worth? We can try and prove ourselves to others, but we are the ones driving the boat at all times. We are the only ones able to slow or stop it completely.

As we struggle to keep up appearances with people, we find ourselves in a continual language pattern of "I have to." It's a subtle way of saying, "there's no way I can't not do this, I've already pre-decided." The issue with the "have to" mentality is it allows us to remain spiritually lazy, choosing to merely submit to a feeling of needing to do something rather than challenging ourselves or others. The mask of feeling the pressure to validate yourself to others is complicated. "Fit in," "do more," "you're not enough," "everyone feels stressed," "get over it," "it's not a big deal"—these are all demonic tones, pointing not to God, but to Satan. And a tone he's made our ears almost deaf to is you "have to."

Living With the Pressure to Prove Leads to I "Have To" and Sin

In the past, I lived on lists. I made them and would check things off, line by line. Part of that was the organizer in me, the ability to stay focused and on task. Lists also gave clarity to where I was trying to go and what I wanted to accomplish. That said, I also leveraged these lists as a way to feel accomplished and valued in my day. I remember a number of times bragging to myself how I'd accomplished twenty or thirty tasks in a day. It was driven by pride. I wanted to get a lot accomplished, and the main way I knew how to quantify my value was by how much I could get done. It was centered on image and pride.

After God showed me this, and I began working on it, I've come to realize that the same habit is back, but it has a new twist to it. It sounds less like pride and more like I "had to" or I "needed to." To be honest, as a stay-at-home mom, I can often find myself in a place where I do things I feel I "have to" do because I'm not bringing in any paycheck. So instead of asking for help, I power through thinking in the back of my head, "The value you add to this family is what you can do, so your husband can just relax when he gets off work." My husband never expressed this, and if anything, is always trying to help take things off my plate, but that doesn't change what I hear at times. Instead of breaking away from imposed demands, many of us are doing things out of a place of feeling like we "have to." What are you currently doing because you think you "have to?"

Doing things because we feel we have to brings a few key things to the surface, especially the sin of pride. Pride manifests in believing everything will fall apart if you don't do it. It's "me" focused. When we live in this place, it causes us to find ourselves boasting about what we accomplished in a day, versus what God did through us. That's a huge shift. We get the credit, or He gets the credit. There's no fifty-fifty option.

It also exposes our sin of people-pleasing instead of God-pleasing. We begin to feel like we can't disappoint anyone, all the while neglecting and rejecting God before us. People-pleasing can become an idol in our lives, and while we are called to love our neighbor and to submit to leaders, we aren't called to obey them before God or put them on a pedestal.

What I've noticed in my own life as I people-please is that I neglect prayer, time with God, fasting, or even approaching him in worship. My focus now becomes, "I have to get this done for _____, then I'll come to you Father. I'll bring you whatever I have left over."

We do it often and don't even realize the impact it's having on us. That's why many of us get nervous when we think about saying no to something we feel we "have to" do. We've been living for so long on this refined version of sugar called "pleasing others first" that we've almost come to crave the taste. It's actually somewhat satisfying when we do it. Why? Because it's familiar, and it's what we know. We can grasp it, but it's also a place where we feel proud of ourselves. It sounds sick, I know, but it's true.

If we confess our sins, he is faithful and just and will forgive us our sins and purify us from all unrighteousness.
1 John 1:9, NIV

We grasp that we have sin in our lives, but don't make it a continual point to confess those sins before God or, at times, before others. Living an authentic life means being restored back to a right relationship with God. God and sin don't mix. Jesus and sin don't mix. The Holy Spirit and sin don't mix. In order for us to be released from our masks, it requires our awareness and repentance of sin. This gives the Holy Trinity (Father, Son, and Holy Spirit) the ability to act on our behalf.

Feeling the pressure to prove to others and ourselves is a mask that many of us pick up in the morning and put on. We fake emotions, we fake the position of our hearts, we fake finances, we fake our relationships with the Father, and all the while feel more stressed out and fearful than ever. God wants you to not respond out of a pressure to perform or prove. There is nothing you can offer Him that Jesus has not already done in His life on earth or on the cross. Living authentically according to God's standards requires you to stop trying so hard to prove something you already are.

We can know the Lord's authentic plan, we can acknowledge that He has more for us, but if we continue to put on the masks of living overscheduled and feeling the pressure to prove, we will remain stagnant in our walk with Him. We will cap what He can do with us, not because He's unable, but because we are unwilling. Taking off the masks of the world is just the first step to living authentically. Now let's jump into the good stuff.

AUTHENTIC

PART TWO: GOD'S AUTHENTIC PLAN

Now that we are aware of what we've been using to cover up, we need to know what God's authentic plans are for us. Authentic is defined as: Made or done the same way as an original.[4] These chapters will serve as a reminder of what we are to be anchored in as believers of Jesus Christ.

AUTHENTIC

GOD'S AUTHENTIC PLAN:
The Gospel

One major gap I see today with believers is an inability to share the gospel of Jesus. In many ways, people feel they can't share or they don't feel qualified to share. We have been able to hide behind pastors and evangelists as the sole careers of the gospel. But God wants you and I to become so passionate about the transformation we've experienced through Jesus Christ, that we can't help but share.

If I were to ask you to tell me what the gospel was in your own words, what would you say? Actually, pause and walk through how you'd describe the gospel to a stranger. I'd encourage you to grab something you can write on and take a few moments to reflect.

A few years back, I was convicted because I didn't know how to share the gospel. I wasn't sure what to leave in and what to leave out. I remember talking to my friend Tasha about it on her sofa, one afternoon. That day, we watched videos on how to share the gospel and spent some time talking through it. The reality was I was coming in contact with my very ignorance. While I'd known Jesus for many years, I didn't know how to communicate His message of hope, life, and reconciliation. And I wasn't okay with that.

I'd sat in church many, many times and heard the gospel message, but just because you hear something doesn't mean you're equipped to share it or that it's translated to your heart. I was spending time with God recently and felt a nudge that hearing is a spiritual revelation, more than a physical one. Hearing God and His word should cause a change in heart. It's easy to physically listen to the message of the gospel and remain unchanged. It happens everyday, people hear the good news and reject it. The gospel if heard in your heart will cause you to forgive yourself and others. It will bring about the fruit of the spirit and life. When we listen with our hearts, we hear differently.

The gospel is the central heartbeat of our walk with God. We can't live authentically in any other area if we don't believe in the power of the gospel. The gospel is crucial, not optional. How often do you share the gospel with people? Do you think it's your responsibility to share? What inhibits you from sharing the gospel?

What is the Gospel?

The gospel, in short, is the reconciliation of us to God. It's sharing about the many ways that God has given us a chance to turn from our sins and come back into a right relationship with Him. It's sharing the good news of Jesus Christ. For some of us, we may be trying to use our testimony as the gospel. In fact, you may have defined it above using your testimony as part of the description. Your testimony is powerful; it's how you were reconciled to God, but it is not the gospel. A person's testimony can include God and yet not express Jesus or his atonement for sin.

When we share the gospel, we are sharing about the written Word of God, the truth of the scriptures. It does not add in personal opinion or perspective but should be pulled directly from scripture. I believe it's important to make sure you're preparing at all times because you never know when you'll have the chance to share the gospel with someone.

I'd personally describe the gospel to another as, after forming the heavens and the Earth, God created man in His own image. He put Adam and Eve in the Garden of Eden, gave them authority, and asked them to care for the garden. He commanded them not to eat of the tree of the knowledge of good and evil, or they would die.

Satan came in disguise as a snake to Eve and tempted her and got her to question the Word of God. Eve took fruit from the tree God commanded not to, ate it, and gave it to her husband Adam. As soon as they ate, their eyes were opened and sin entered the world. Since that moment, man has been struggling with sin.

God has always desired to be in a relationship with us. That's why He created us. But, being the holy and sinless God He is, sin separated us from Him. So in the Old Testament, animals used to be sacrificed for the atonement of sin. But people kept sinning over and over again. So in His great love for us, God sent His Son Jesus. Jesus was both God and man and was born to Mary and Joseph. He was the ultimate and final sacrifice for all sin. No more animals were to be sacrificed, instead, a Messiah came.

Jesus lived a sinless life, obeyed the commandments of God, and died on the cross. His death was required to fulfill the law that was written. After dying, He was buried and rose again in three days. He later ascended into heaven and is seated at the right hand of the Father. Scripture tells us if we believe and profess with our mouths that Jesus Christ is Lord and that He came, died, was buried, and rose from the grave, we will be saved. Not by our works or other sacrifices, but by faith in the blood of Jesus Christ.

Knowing the gospel is only the first step in the process, once we know it we have to be willing to share it with others. We all have a responsibility to share about Jesus. For what good is it to keep the good news all to ourselves?

Our Responsibility to Share the Gospel

Sharing what we believe in is hard. In fact, I think many times, we steer away from it because it brings up uncomfortable tension, and even possibly elicits questions from others to which we don't feel we have the answers. So, we cower away from sharing at all. That's a tactic of the enemy, to silence the gospel, to silence us. You do know that we are the only ones able to get the gospel out at this current time in history. God chose to create you and me, not to just exist, but to live a life on purpose both sharing and living out the gospel.

He said to them, 'Go into all the world and preach the gospel to all creation.'
Mark 16:15, NIV

Again Jesus said, 'Peace be with you! As the Father has sent me, I am sending you.'
John 20:21, NIV

I pray that your partnership with us in the faith may be effective in deepening your understanding of every good thing we share for the sake of Christ.
Philemon 1:6, NIV

He told them, 'The harvest is plentiful, but the workers are few. Ask the Lord of the harvest, therefore, to send out workers into his harvest field.'
Luke 10:2, NIV

Luke 10:2 speaks to the reality of modern-day society. Jesus was alluding to the fact that there are many people who need to come to the saving knowledge of Jesus Christ. But there are few followers of Him that are willing to do the work. Are you a worker?

Being a worker doesn't mean just sharing the gospel when it fits your schedule or is convenient but doing it when God says to. A worker is focused on the labor that God has before them, even if it's inconvenient. The gospel, at times, is inconvenient. Paul wasn't told to share the gospel where he was well-liked but where he was told to go. Peter, Andrew, James, and John were asked to leave everything to follow Jesus. There was no insurance plan to fall back on in case the gospel wasn't easy to share.

We long for security. We fight for comfort. The danger is that when we feel we are experiencing these things, we don't feel a need for God or Jesus in our lives. To not only live out the gospel but share it will require us to let go of our control and comfort, or should I say our illusion of it.

In 2020, our world experienced the start of a pandemic. Likely, as you read over those words, thoughts and memories rush to your mind. It was a time that taught us we can plan all we want, but we can't control everything. It created discomfort for many and made it clear why the gospel is still so necessary. If you think I'm merely talking about guaranteeing eternity in heaven alone, you have missed it. People needed hope in 2020; people needed joy and peace when they were turning on the news, only to be hit once more with shortages, virus deaths, and racial divide. People needed love when they felt isolated and alone. People needed Jesus, here on Earth. I'm so thankful that the gospel isn't just about later but about right now, that it's about healing right now, that it's about mercy right now. We all are responsible for sharing the gospel, not later, not only when it feels right, but right now.

I know it's easy to get hung up on how to communicate the gospel. We can often over complicate the process, forgetting that the good news does its own work. We don't have to worry about figuring it all out, we just have to worry about taking the next step.

It Does its Own Work

Recently, my husband and I were having a conversation. Things were getting a bit heated, at least on my side. I was speaking about the gospel and about how there is no more wavering. You have to choose to either accept Jesus and the Word of God fully or not. There is no bouncing back and forth. I remember that it hit me, the gospel does its own work. Meaning, the gospel is both love and truth, I don't have to do all the work for it. I don't have to feel I need to coddle someone when it comes to the reality of the Word of God, because the Word itself is both salt and light, it's gentle and it rebukes.

One of the real tensions we have in this world as believers is how to not only share the gospel but also feeling like we have to try to make sure that it is chewable. I'll never forget one random conversation I had with a neighbor. He said, "here in America, the church is feeding people baby food, but eventually people have to grow up and learn how to eat big people's food instead of sucking on a bottle for nourishment." He was referencing 1 Corinthians 3:2. This struck me. I was actually taken aback by his statement. He and his wife were from Ghana. How they experienced life and God was far different than here in the Western world. But what still sticks with me is his analogy between a bottle and liquid nourishment versus having the physical ability and digestive ability to process food.

When we share about Jesus with others, I think most of us lean more toward the milk side of things. We want to make sure we don't make the other person feel uncomfortable. Here's the problem with that: Who's the gospel about? Jesus. Yes, Jesus came to save us, but the gospel is about HIM. So if we are trying to water down the gospel so that people can drink it, and specifically cater it more to them than Jesus, that is a problem. The gospel was never intended to not be offensive.

I know the gospel, at times, feels like it's all-inclusive, but the gospel was and is intended to separate, to sift, to break apart those who follow the Son and those who don't. The signs and miracles we read about in the Bible sound amazing to us, but they were offensive, hard pieces of steak to chew for people at that time. It wasn't easy. You either had to choose: Did you believe Jesus to be the Messiah or did you believe Him to be working for Satan? There was no spoon-feeding. I'm not implying by any means that we need to force the gospel on people and tell them to accept it or go to hell. But many of us have come to a place where we are quicker to try and comfort another person so they don't feel offended about the Word of God, than to stay anchored in the Word of God, knowing He's always first.

A great question to ask yourself is this: "If I was asked to share about Jesus with another person I didn't know, would I try and water the Word of God down to make myself feel more comfortable or would I speak the truth, even if it made me feel uncomfortable?" Notice I didn't say "them" but "myself." We make excuses many times and pin the blame on others when, in actuality, it is something we are wrestling with. Part of the reason you may think you need to make others feel comfortable about the gospel is that you are uncomfortable with it. You're uncomfortable sharing it because you don't know how. You're uncomfortable sharing it because you care more about what they will think of you after it than being obedient to God. You're uncomfortable sharing it because you actually don't care about the gospel because your eternity is set, so who cares about anyone else? You're uncomfortable, so you sit and do nothing or you try to liquefy the truth. I'm guilty of this too. Please don't think I've arrived.

I don't want you to feel condemned by this, but I do think it's important to discuss, to be honest with where we actually are, and to address the areas in our faith that may be lacking or causing us to doubt. All these things impact not just our ability but desire to not only share the gospel but live it. God is not looking at you upset but eager. Eager to see you grow and get hungry for the things of His heart.

I know that in my own life, I've realized there have been many areas where I tended to lean toward grace instead of speaking truth; areas in my walk with God, Jesus, and the Holy Spirit that I watered down with others because it was easier.

To water something down is: to reduce or temper the force or effectiveness of.[5]

Watering anything down makes it weaker, not as strong as in its original form. It causes the food or drink to lose its flavor, texture, and nutrients. We cannot water down the gospel. The gospel is about the saving grace of Jesus Christ. We can't leave out parts of the Word of God that will offend others; we can't turn the Word of God into the word that makes us feel comfortable and happy. That's not God at all.

The responsibility of the gospel of Jesus Christ belongs to all of us, not just one man or woman who stands on a stage on Sunday for sixty minutes a week. Not just one person who is in the mission field abroad. Not just one individual who is leading a Christian non-profit. But it is the great commission (Matthew 28:16-20) of all who follow Jesus.

It's time we carry the gospel with us to the people God's placed in our lives. It is time now to go and share about the hope and love of Jesus. It is time now, in our homes, jobs, churches, and friend circles to share about Jesus. Don't know where to start? Maybe set a goal this week to write out and practice sharing the gospel. Next week, plan to meet up with a friend and practice sharing it with one another and maybe even practice how you could share it in different situations. I was telling my husband that we plan and prepare for fleeting things but rarely plan and prepare for God's things.

Just as we would plan and prepare for an emergency in our

finances, we should prepare for the Kingdom of God. But let me let you in on a little secret, it's already here and now! And it's more valuable than gold.

AUTHENTIC

GOD'S AUTHENTIC PLAN:
Rest

When I say the word rest, what comes to mind? Would you say rest is something you desire more of in your life? I've noticed in my own life that it's easy to desire something but it's often difficult to actually change things to align with what's desired. Rest has always been a tough one for me and it appears to be increasingly difficult for many in our world today. This chapter is all about you realizing the untapped potential of rest you have access to. It's more than a weekend off to God, it's more than a shabbat dinner to God, it's a continual state that He desires for us to live in.

Where I think many people get hung up when it comes to rest is that it's viewed in one of three ways. One, rest is Friday when you get off until Sunday and it's me focused. Two, the Sabbath isn't a Holy day or about resting in the Lord. Three, rest is optional and not necessarily needed. Where we originate our mindset on these things likely impacts how we actually experience rest.

"Me" Focused Weekend

Have you ever met a person who is me-focused? When you talk, they constantly want to tell you how they're doing and what's new in their life. They don't even stop to ask how you're doing or what's new. Their focus is on one thing, themselves. When it comes to a Friday to Sunday rest habit apart from God, it is me-focused. The places I spend my time, where I spend my money and energy, are all centered on what pleases me.

Now, this is a dangerous place to be because if the focus for why someone does something is self-centered, their measurement scale is themselves. Rest that is not Biblically based is me-based. By having a Friday to Sunday perspective on rest, you can limit the other four days of the week. God desires for us to experience rest in our daily lives.

In Luke 5, we read about how Jesus heals a man from leprosy. He was at work. After he heals the man he commands him not to tell anyone and Luke records that, "Jesus often withdrew to lonely places and prayed" (Luke 5:16, NIV). A place where we can consistently access rest is through prayer. I don't want to dig too much into this, as we will be discussing it in our next chapter, but I want to introduce the thought that living a lifestyle of continual rest is possible if we exercise prayer more regularly throughout our day. Prayer shifts our eyes from us, to God. From our situations that are stressing us out, to a peace in our Lord.

It's important to remember that rest is labeled holy by God. Meaning, it's not common or just a happenstance, but it is set apart and significant. Therefore when we make rest about what we can do to recharge ourselves apart from God, we miss the very purpose of rest. Rest is a holy gift that many of us are not accessing.

Sabbath isn't a Holy day

By the seventh day God had finished the work he had been doing; so on the seventh day he rested from all his work. Then God blessed the seventh day and made it holy, because on it he rested from all the work of creating that he had done.
Genesis 2:2-3, NIV

How do you define Sabbath? Do you set aside one day a week to intentionally rest with God and your family? Sabbath is a break from all working one day a week. During Jesus' time, it was celebrated from sundown Friday night to Saturday night. Sabbath is a time to rest as a family, worship God, and cease physical labor. It serves as a reminder of who God is and what His Word says. The focus of the Sabbath is God first, then me. Sabbath is regarded as such a significant part of who we are that it's the fourth of the Ten Commandments God gave Moses.

Remember the Sabbath day by keeping it holy. Six days you shall labor and do all your work, but the seventh day is a sabbath to the Lord your God. On it you shall not do any work, neither you, nor your son or daughter, nor your male or female servant, nor your animals, nor any foreigner residing in your towns. For in six days the Lord made the heavens and the earth, the sea, and all that is in them, but he rested on the seventh day. Therefore the Lord Blessed the Sabbath day and made it holy.
Exodus 20:8-11, NIV

More often than not, I see Christians emulating their peers, not taking time to stop and practice Sabbath. While we say we want things in our lives, like rest, it requires discipline to actually carry it out on a consistent basis. God gave us rest as a gift, to stop and slow down, to get a breather, a reprieve. Think about it this way. Have you ever deleted social media off your phone or gone without your phone for hours? If you have, you would likely say it was freeing. It decreases stress and distraction and lets you be present in the moment. You were no longer mindlessly clicking that app and beginning the continual swiping through of moments. You felt so free not having your texts go off, putting you in a constant state of alert. When we take a Sabbath, it's like removing those things but way better. It reminds us of the peace and love our Father has for us. It serves as a reminder that the things we actually think are important pale in comparison.

One of the things I've come to love about Sabbath is the time we get together as a family. We've worked really hard to talk through and plan a specific and intentional Sabbath time. From Shabbat dinners to family fun day activities. I will try and prepare the meals for the day in advance and have a no-cleaning policy. For us, it's about spending time with God and refueling as a unit and individually. My husband loves to golf, so sometimes he'll go out to the driving range, and I love to cook, so sometimes I'll learn a new recipe or try something I've been wanting to learn. I've had to remind myself over and over again that Sabbath is not an option, it's a command. And it was always a part of God's authentic plan for my life.

Rest is Optional

Do you live a life where you believe rest is optional? Does the thought of rest bring you to worry or anxiety, because you think you could miss something or don't know how to live in stillness?

In life, it's easy to classify things as optional. From how I take care of my body, to where I live, to what I drive, life can feel like it's full of options. And in one sense, that's true, we have free will. But there are consequences to choosing the wrong options.

When I first became a follower of Christ, I didn't understand the concept of rest. I also didn't learn about it, so I didn't practice Sabbath. It was optional. In fact, I made most of my money on the weekends so I found myself always working. Side note, Sabbath doesn't have to happen from Friday to Saturday. You can honor the Lord any day, it just needs to be intentional.

While I wasn't educated on the Sabbath, I also would have likely still worked at the time had I known. I say this because I openly admit, at the time, money had a huge grip on my life. It was an idol. It was the place I put my trust in being able to survive, not God. I have a feeling that, for some of you, part of not observing Sabbath and resting hinges on the sin of what role money plays in your life. You want to make money because you find value, status, and things in it that you don't believe a Sabbath can give you. You want more of everything else but God. The one thing I'd forgotten while toiling for money was that God was the one determining what ultimately ended up in my hands.

Sabbath rest in the church is another area that, at times, I have seen a lack of boundaries. God obviously loves His church, His people, and His body. And the church will never be a perfect place, but we should always be growing and developing in righteous living. That being said, if you are feeling pressured to serve and be at so many church events that it inhibits your ability to practice a Sabbath, that's not God's way. God established rest before the church. I see too many people running around in the church at all sorts of events, serving Sundays, and at leader meetings. Yet, at home, they aren't setting a standard for what living a lifestyle of rest is, things are at odds with their spouse, and they are burnt out from feeling uncared for.
Serving in the church isn't bad, going to the event isn't bad, and leader meetings aren't bad. But we are first called to obey and have a relationship with God through Jesus. And part of that relationship includes rest. It's easier, though, to have a relationship at my local church because it keeps my calendar full like I'm used to, and I can feel a sense of instant gratification.

This is what the Lord says:
'Stand at the crossroads and look;
ask *for the ancient paths,*
ask *where the good way is, and walk in it,*
and you will find rest for your souls.'
But you said, 'We will not walk in it.'
Jeremiah 6:16, NIV, emphasis added

If you're someone who considers rest optional, odds are there are many things at play. I like this verse from Jeremiah because the Lord is saying to ask for direction when it comes to rest, and you will find it. But, you also have to choose to walk in it. That's really the epitome of our faith. We learn from Jesus and choose to either live a righteous life mimicking Him as our example or ignore what we've been taught.

What led so often to Jesus' rest in scriptures was His love for His father. Because he loved God and felt loved by him, he remained steadfast and obedient to resting in God. Rest is a love issue. We don't observe rest, nor see its value, if we don't seek it as a way to express our love to God and be loved by God.

Loved

When you think of the word love, what comes to mind? When I think of love, I think of Jesus, how He loves me so much, how He desires for me to know Him more, how He reveals Himself to me in His Words, how He's been playful with me at moments, how He's held me during some of my toughest days, and how He's fought for me when I didn't want to fight for myself. Jesus is what I think about first when I think of love. Yet, in the same breath, I also think I'm not fully worthy of His love. I'm not good enough to receive the love He desires to give me. This can bleed into rest because instead of resting in the fact that Jesus has already made me enough before God and man, I continue striving, filling my precious hours of rest with doing.

Love is a powerful word. Love impacts the way we see others, ourselves, and how we rest. We were innately created to feel love.

However, as it is written:
'What no eye has seen,

> *what no ear has heard,*
> *and what no human mind has conceived'—*
> *the things God has prepared for those who love him.*
> 1 Corinthians 2:9, NIV

One of the most precious things being stolen from us with our rest, is our secret place with God. Instead of having an appetite for silence, stillness, and revelation from God alone we can become anxious about the very thought of being still and quiet. We're afraid to be alone with the One who loves us most. I remember when I first started practicing silence and stillness with God, it was hard. It still is hard sometimes. There are always things trying to compete for God's rightful lordship in our life. But sitting and resting in Christ has a way of changing us. It has a way of showing us how much we are loved. It is a way to show our devotion to God and adoration for Him. When our desire for God's presence increases, our ability to be present with our families increases. It's a transferable asset.

Odds are if you are struggling to be still with God and rest, you are struggling to be still and rest with your family, friends, or spouse. When we understand and truly believe that we are loved by God, just as we are, our rest becomes more accessible. We become more willing to stop and receive or give thanks, instead of continuing in our chaotic ways. Stopping for a Sabbath becomes something to look forward to, not something to dread.

You may be walking in alignment with God in many other areas of your life, but when it comes to rest, you're completely off. The longer you walk in the wrong direction, the longer it will take to return back to the original place God intended for you.

I used to hate multiple-choice questions on tests. I hated them because you got multiple options that kind of sounded similar and were meant to confuse you. I remember taking my SAT in the cafeteria at Dacula High School . . . so many multiple-choice questions. Hopefully, you have a better relationship with multiple-choice questions than I did, because I want to ask you one.

> What is your current relationship with rest?
> a) I do rest, by practicing a Sabbath and resting in the Lord daily.
> b) I don't rest.
> c) I do rest, but I long for more.
> d) I don't think rest is a value in my life right now.
> e) I don't rest because I'm not sure how to be still with God.

It may seem funny, but the answer to the question has the ability to get you to a place of freedom. The reality is, you may still be looking at the options and saying, I actually live a different answer than I want to circle. I have good news, Jesus can help. In fact, He's great at resting; go check out Mark 6:31-32.

I know rest is highly undervalued in our society. At times, it can even be labeled as a weakness or as laziness if someone lives by it. But God created us to live in a space of rest. It was His authentic plan. You and I have a choice, just like with anything else in life. We can choose to embrace rest and discipline ourselves or we can ignore it. But may I just remind you, God is madly in love with you. And in God's generosity and love for us, He wants us to rest. Rest on His Sabbath, rest because we know we're loved, rest daily, and mostly rest in the finished work of Jesus on the cross.

AUTHENTIC

GOD'S AUTHENTIC PLAN:
Prayer

Are you intimidated to pray? I'm opening with a hard question, I know. But prayer unlocks many things and we must not be intimidated to step into the battlefield. I call it a battlefield because it is an area of our walk with God that allows us access to the spiritual realm. It gives us a seat at the table to play an active role with the angels through intercession. We get to co-labor alongside them and see the victory. Prayer is the main way we communicate with God. If we are going to live authentically, we will have to not only learn to pray, but not be intimidated by it.

When God created man and woman in the Garden, in His image, He was in communication with them directly. We know this because in Genesis, we witness direct dialogue between God and man.

Then the man and his wife heard the sound of the Lord God as he was walking in the garden in the cool of the day, and they hid from the Lord God among the trees of the garden. But the Lord God called to the man, 'Where are you?' He answered, 'I heard you in the garden, and I was afraid because I was naked; so I hid.'
Genesis 3:8-10, NIV

The Lord goes on in dialogue with both Adam and Eve. He asks them questions and listens for their response. It's funny because even here in scripture, we know that God already knew the answers that they were going to give, but wanted to hear them say it. After being banished from the Garden, for our sins, we have no longer been able to physically see our Lord. We are told many times in scripture including from Jesus, that we pray to a Father that is unseen. We went from direct communication and an ability to see the Lord, to direct communication and not being able to see the Lord. Our access to the Lord has not changed, merely our ability to physically see Him.

And while we may not be able to see our Lord physically, we are able to see Him spiritually, through prayer. Prayer is the place where we get to have our Father speak back to us, as he did to Adam and Eve in the Garden. We have no reason to be intimidated or afraid as we approach God in prayer, He already knows what we need and God loves when we come before Him in humility and simplicity of prayer. God desires to hear your voice, there's none like it. To Him the greatest gift you can give Him as a believer of Jesus Christ is a continual desire to want to speak to Him.

That should take off some of the weight you've been unintentionally placing on yourself, to come before God as perfect. There is only one who is perfect and our Father sees him when He looks at us.

He Knows What You Need

I think part of the intimidation process in prayer is the vocalizing of what is in our hearts, or what we perceive we need. There's something about saying what you think that can at times make you feel a bit unholy or greedy. Vocalizing to God what we desire can at times feel exhausting because we've been asking Him for the same thing for years. And instead of bringing it before the Father in prayer, Satan desires for us to let it sit. If it sits it can fester and grow roots of bitterness or disappointment.

There have been times in my life where anger or unforgiveness have sat. I knew I needed to bring it to God in prayer, or to others in an act of repentance. But I was unwilling to listen to the prompt. It became this festering, leaving me more angry and bitter than I was before. I love that Proverbs says:

Can a man scoop fire into his lap without his clothes being burned?
Can a man walk on hot coals without his feet being scorched?
Proverbs 6:27-28, NIV

Can we idly sit with sin within our hearts and not expect to get scorched? Prayer is both a revealing place, but also a healing place. I want to encourage you that the Father already knows what's there. It's not a surprise to Him. He's been waiting for you to bring your worries, pain, or bitterness to Him, even if it is about Him. He can handle it. We forget that God is holding the Universe in perfect harmony, so I think He can handle your frustration or anger towards Him.

I love that God clothed Adam and Even in the Garden even after their sin. They vocalize to God that they betrayed Him and that they sinned. And in their own efforts made clothes out of leaves. They had come up with the solution to the problem without bringing it to their Father first. How many times has this been you and I, apart from prayer? I love that we serve a God that says, even though you hurt me, even though you fell short, even though you disobeyed my commands, I want you to wear something better. Something more durable, more valuable. We should never be afraid to come to our Father in prayer.

Regardless of what you need to lay before God in prayer, know that it's not too big for His love to cover. God's not expecting us to do some grand gesture in our prayers to show Him our words have value, but instead to be honest and vulnerable with where we are. God desires a simple prayer from His sons and daughters. A prayer of directness and truth. God wants to clothe you and I in something new, but if we don't communicate with Him, how can he?

Start Simple, Then Build

When I first became a believer I remember setting a timer for five minutes on my phone to pray. I had a goal to pray that whole time and because prayer was new to me, I had to start somewhere. I remember looking around my room and thanking God for the shirts in my closet, my furniture, my lamps, anything I could lay my eyes on. The reality was that I didn't know exactly how to pray, but I did know I needed it to be a part of my life.

And while we can desire to pray more, we may not know exactly where to start. A foundational step to simple prayer that all of us can take is memorizing the Lord's prayer. If you have never memorized it, I would encourage you to do so over the days and weeks to come. This is the only prayer that Jesus directly taught the disciples and we find it in Matthew 6: 9-13 (NIV):

> This, then, is how you should pray:
> *Our Father in heaven,*
> *hallowed be your name,*
> *your kingdom come,*
> *your will be done,*
> *on earth as it is in heaven.*
> *Give us today our daily bread.*
> *And forgive us our debts,*
> *as we also have forgiven our debtors.*
> *And lead us not into temptation*
> *but deliver us from the evil one.*

The prayer encompasses much, but is simply five verses. As believers in Jesus, we should all know the Lord's prayer. The Lord's prayer invites us into trusting the Lord daily and reminds us of our continual desperation for His son.

Jesus showed us not just in Matthew, but time and time again in scripture that prayer was a continual part of his everyday life. Jesus prayed without ceasing. There was a burning desire within Jesus to stay in communication with his love, God the Father. It wasn't a task to him. It wasn't hard to want to meet his Father in conversation. Praying without ceasing was Jesus' refreshment and reminder of the mission. The idea of Jesus praying without ceasing seems simple, but often the most simple things in life can be the things we take for granted.

Pray Without Ceasing

Rejoice always, pray continually, give thanks in all circumstances; for this is God's will for you in Christ Jesus.
1 Thessalonians 5:16-18, NIV

When you think about praying to God, likely the words "without ceasing" don't come to mind. Paul is encouraging us here, to always have prayer on our lips. A continual state of praising, thanking, and making our request known to God is necessary. There is no stopping or ending point with our prayer. It's easy to see prayer as something to check off. Like reading our Bible we can have a narrow mindset that we need to only exercise our relationship with these things once a day. But continual prayer without ceasing is the heart of Christ.

Let me present it like this. I want you to think about the person you talk to on average the most in a day. It could be a spouse, friend, co-worker, or family member. Now if you were to cut your communication with them down to a once a day talk, what would that relationship look like? If you're merely talking to them to check it off the list. Odds are, things wouldn't be too hot. In fact we can live in friendships and marriages that resemble this very thing. A transactional relationship that meets the bottom line commitments. But the Lord loves us so much that he wants us to continually be in communication with Him.

It doesn't have to be long or drawn out, in fact Jesus warns about that being disingenuous. God just wants to know that we are thinking about Him, desiring Him, and excited to share what's on our hearts with Him, not just once a day, but many times a day. Remember prayer is our access point to the battle. So if we feel in the middle of our day like we are riddled with worry, that's our opportunity to stop and pray. It gives us access to change the situation or our perspective of it. We get to pick up our sword of truth and speak not to what we feel, but to who God is. Prayer is a gift and it grants us Garden access to the Father. While we may not be able to see God, he hears us, and if we lean in and listen, we can hear Him too.

> Prayer is not a task or a to do, but a continual conversation between us and the Father.
>
> Prayer is not something to cower away from or be afraid of, but where we get to acknowledge our sins, repent, and heal.
>
> Prayer is not to be perfected with eloquent words lacking heart, but where we are to remain simple and genuine.
>
> Prayer is not the last resort, but the first one.

Communication has always been a part of God's authentic plan for His people. Since the foundations of the world, God has desired to hear our voice, our cries, our struggles. We were made in God's image not just to resemble Him, but to desire intimate, continual relationship with Him. And no relationship is possible without communication.

AUTHENTIC

GOD'S AUTHENTIC PLAN:
Engaging with the Father through His Word

Reading has never been a strong suit for me. Even as a child, it was not something I enjoyed. I would often feel embarrassed when I couldn't pronounce certain words and would quickly become discouraged. However, there were a few books that I so loved, I'd find myself reading them time and time again. One of those books was James and the Giant Peach. I loved the book because I just seemed to get lost in it. It was fun, it was intriguing, and it was simple yet complicated.

I find the Word of God to be all those things too, but also so much more. It's encouragement, love, correction, conviction, truth, relevant, forward-focused, and can expose the past and future. God created us to authentically be in a relationship with Him, and one of the ways we experience that relationship is through His Word. I know that when I became a believer, there were no classes to explain how to read or study God's Word, so I learned over many years. I'm excited to hopefully share some ways to read and study the Bible that helped me along the way. I will start by saying these are not the only ways to do it. We serve a God who is so creative, He made millions and billions of different types of people. So God can speak in many ways as well. If you've found a way to experience God in His Word that has worked for you, I couldn't be more excited for you. I'd encourage you to write it out and pray that God would give you someone that you can share it with.

I believe reading and studying the Bible is one of the most fulfilling things you can do, and it creates an opportunity for direct access to the Father. So if you're reading this and you are in a funk with your quiet time with God, or possibly, you just don't even know where to begin, I'm excited to go on this journey with you. I believe reading the Word of God isn't about arriving at a place. I know the world tries to tell us we need to arrive at all these markers in our life, as though significance comes from achieving some end goal. But when it comes to God, He is forever a part of our story; we are merely on a journey with Him in discovering who He's made us to be. And one of the places I've gotten to learn more about the Bible and who God's made me to be, is in small groups.

Small groups are one of my favorite things in church. Maybe because it makes a large church feel small, maybe because it's nice to just find people who are real and can challenge you, maybe because I just love doing ministry with people in homes. During one of my women's small groups in Charlotte, North Carolina, one of the young ladies shared that she felt discouraged about her time in the Word of God. She felt she wasn't sure where to begin, so she found herself reading Bible App verses and a quick devotional daily.

I believe devotionals and the Bible app verses for the day are great tools, but they aren't possible without the real thing, the Word of God. They aren't a substitute; they aren't God's Word in full. I want to bring this up because it's easy for us to try and sustain ourselves on something that isn't fully the word of God. Even this very book, while based on the word of God, lacks the ability to sustain you, encourage you, or transform you long term.

When we substitute the word of God for quick devotions and verses of the day it's like going to Ruth's Chris Steak House and ordering a steak with broccoli and potatoes. The steak is the main course; it's the reason you went to Ruth's Chris. If all you eat when it comes out are the potatoes and broccoli, then you're going to be really disappointed and likely still hungry. Why? Because you came for steak, for nourishment. The Word of God is complete nourishment. You don't go to Ruth's Chris for broccoli and potatoes, you go for the steak.

We can miss the substance of the Bible not only when we replace it with cheap devotionals, but also when we **don't** remember to focus more on the quality of what we are reading than the quantity, when we **don't** read with time and space, when we **don't** bring a pen and journal to write down revelation, and when we **don't** utilize prayer in the process. These four areas have become key in transforming my quiet time.

Read Not for Quantity but Quality

When I first became a Christian, I began reading my Bible, thinking it was about accomplishing an assignment. But remember, as I said above, reading the Bible is not about arriving somewhere but about going on a journey. I wanted to read as much of the Bible as I could, as fast as I could. When you read the Word of God, my first encouragement is to read not for quantity but for quality. God is not expecting us to read a certain amount each time we open His Word, so take a deep breath. God knows that while He is the same yesterday and today, we are not. When we put pressure on ourselves to read as much of the Bible as possible in the shortest amount of time, we can find ourselves in a legalistic mindset.

If God calls you to read the Bible in a year, do it. We always need to be sold out to obedience. And there are seasons for consuming the word of God at a rapid pace, but don't put pressure or a standard on yourself to accomplish something if God never spoke it. Part of our worldly culture says accomplish, accomplish, accomplish. And if we're not careful, we will not only see it manifest in our work life, home life, parenting life, and schedule, but we will also find it overlaps in our relationship with God.

Since you died with Christ to the elemental spiritual forces of this world, why, as though you still belonged to the world, **do you submit to its rules***: "Do not handle! Do not taste! Do not touch!"* **These rules, which have to do with things that are all destined to perish with use, are based on merely human commands and teachings. Such regulations indeed have an appearance of wisdom, with their self-imposed worship, their false humility and their harsh treatment of the body, but they lack any value in restraining sensual indulgence.**
Colossians 2:20-23, NIV, emphasis added

I love that Paul is saying they have the "appearance of wisdom." Reading as much of your Bible as possible seems like wisdom, but may I implore that the reason God left us the Bible is not so we could consume information, but so we could enter into a relationship with Him and change the way we live. His Words are intended to speak to us. But we have to realize it's not about quantity but quality. Reading with the intention of quality changes not only our perspective on why we're reading, it also changes how much time we're willing to devote to it. We are often more willing to invest time into things that we find to be beneficial or life giving to us. And God's word is both of those things.

Read With Time and Space

Rush. Rush. Rush. That's what life screams and, to be honest, it can be hard to take a moment and just sit uninterrupted. But when it comes to spending quality time with God, we have to give Him time and space. The more we try to rush through our time with Him, the more likely we are to miss the fullness of what He's trying to say. I've had literal times when my husband was talking to me and all I kept thinking about is what I needed to do around the house. I wasn't able to hear or retain what he said. I've had more moments than I'd like to admit like this, moments where I looked engaged, but my mind was off five days from then. God wants your undivided and focused attention.

Over the years, my time and space with God have changed drastically. When I first became a believer, I was a bartender at Texas Roadhouse in Hiram, Georgia. Because I worked afternoon to night hours, I had all the time I wanted to sit with God. There was no rush to it. But when I moved to Charlotte and took a job at a church, things got complicated. While doing all these things for God, I found my time with God becoming less and less. I began to backslide on my morning time with Him and found myself undisciplined in prioritizing it.

It's important to mention that it wasn't the church's fault. This is not a moment to point fingers. I prioritized doing things for God before spending time with God. I was lacking discipline in some areas of my life, and I take responsibility for that. What I learned was, if you are serving God with your talents and not spending time with Him in His Word, you need to reverse the cycle. He doesn't want things from you before He wants time with you. I speak with far too many believers who say they haven't had time with God because they have been busy with the work of ministry. God came before the church, Jesus came before the church, and we have to make sure we remember that when it comes to our time, too.

Notice I said a word above that pointed the finger at myself: I was undisciplined. Discipline isn't the most comfortable or nice feeling thing for us as humans. We like the results of continued discipline; we just hate having to choose it on a daily basis. If you feel hurried in your time with God, may I ask you a question? How disciplined are you in the time and space you're giving Him? Discipline is all a matter of what you choose to prioritize.

For some of you, you have been blaming your schedule, bosses, and workload on not being able to spend time with God but have yet to say no to other things such as, working extra hours or not leaving ten minutes early to go get that Starbucks drink you must have before work. Giving time and space to God for your quiet time requires a continual pattern of discipline.

God is not rushed. God is not operating in the same twenty-four hours as us. God is not operating with the same worldly pressures as us. And I know we don't have the luxury to call all the things off and just sit with God, we have bills to pay and groceries to buy. But there is space in your schedule to give time to God. I'd recommend thirty minutes for someone new to your faith. Carve out thirty uninterrupted minutes to focus. If you've been a believer for longer, I'd encourage you to pray and ask the Lord what amount of time he'd like from you. For me, currently, my time can vary from thirty minutes to three hours or more.

It's hard to hear what God is saying if we don't make time to listen to Him. But I promise you once you start to make time and hear what God's saying, you'll want more of Him. You'll slowly forget to keep track of how long you've been sitting with God, because you're more wrapped up in what He's speaking to you. And right about then you'll want a pen and journal nearby, because there are things you won't want to miss writing down.

Read With a Pen and Journal Nearby

My friend, Tasha, bought me a Life Application Bible when I was ordained. If you were to look at it, you'd notice how marked up it is. I've written on it with pens of different colors. The margins have notes and questions, verses are underlined and words are circled. I know for some writing in the Bible is taboo, but for me, it is a way I can go back to what God spoke in another season and see it in a different way. It is a place I can come back to remember what was spoken or said by the Father to me.

Having a pen and journal with you during quiet time is key. I'd encourage marking your Bible if you feel comfortable. But if writing in your Bible isn't for you, having a journal nearby to write down what the Lord spoke to you in scripture is huge. That can be anything from a verse to a word, to a question you had from reading the scripture. One of my favorite things to do is to write down what stuck out and then journal on those specific things. When you read and something jumps off the page at you, that is the Holy Spirit speaking to you. Don't brush it off but lean into it. I can't tell you how many times a number or word has stuck out to me and I was completely confused as to why. When that happens, I often go into study mode. You can both read the Bible and journal what it says, but you can also study the Bible. This means you take time to research, read up, and discover the significance of something. Below we are going to walk through a practical example of how to practice studying the Bible.

*Moreover, we will bring to the **storerooms** of the house of our God, to the priests, the first of our ground meal, of our grain offerings, of the fruit of all our trees and of our **new wine** and olive oil. And we will bring a tithe of our crops to the Levites, for it is the Levites who collect the tithes in all the towns where we work. A priest descended from Aaron is to accompany the Levites when they receive the tithes, and the Levites are to bring a tenth of the tithes up to the house of our God, to the **storerooms** of the treasury.*
Nehemiah 10:37-38, NIV, emphasis added

I want to use this scripture as an example. When I read this verse, the words that are bolded are what stand out to me. So, I began to study both words: storerooms and new wine.

Storerooms	New Wine
The place something has been entrusted for a time.	Fresh, new, clean, vibrant.
Other scriptures with storerooms in it: Nehemiah 13:5, Nehemiah 13:7, Matthew 12:35, Luke 12:24	Other scripture with new wine in it: Matthew 9:17
Storeroom is an inner chamber.[6]	New wine was symbolic of Jesus' coming New Kingdom.[7]
Synonyms of Storeroom: safe, vault, treasury.[8]	Representing Christ's blood and the New Covenant.[9]

This is a small chart of research I did to try and study what those words mean. Through my research, I came to realize that what God was trying to tell me is that:

He's entrusting me to store up. I'm His storeroom. He's also doing something new in me; what I used to be is no longer the same. So I can't approach how I spend my time in the same old ways, my relationship with Him through the same old lens, or what He's going to do through me with the same old perspective. He's doing something new.

Each of the words stood out, but it took some studying to really reveal what He was fully saying to me. Having a pen and journal nearby allowed me to capture, on paper, what He spoke. One of the things that I like to do is stop and pray for a moment when I feel like the Lord has given me revelation on something. Expressing my gratitude but also excitement for having eyes to see a little clearer what God was writing to me, is crucial. It not only allows me a chance to process, but it gives me more of a hunger to continue to engage in God's Word.

Start and End With a Prayer Sandwich

I love that Mike Todd's church, Transformation Church, says, "Prayer is the secret sauce." When we pray with our time in God's Word, it gives us a greater depth of understanding and connection. I generally pray for a few moments before starting to read, asking that God would correct me or show me His love through His Word. I also, at times, pray for focus when I really find myself bogged down mentally. It gives me an intentional moment to say, "Lord, I'm excited to enter into this time together. I'm here and I'm listening—speak to me."

If you find that you're distracted while reading God's Word, stop and pray; don't just push through. Occasionally, I'll also stop during my reading if something is hitting me hard and just begin to converse with God, really talking through what was speaking to me and why. It's okay to break the structure at times. There can be this stigma that time with God needs to look a specific way, but ironically, nowhere in the Word do we see a seven-step process to having a "perfect quiet time." Instead, we get to choose. I believe in the moments we break away because we are being led by the Spirit, God rejoices. When we stop reading our Bibles to pray for a neighbor we see, I believe God rejoices. Don't be so glued to the process that you miss the purpose. Closing your time with God in prayer is also something I'd encourage you to do. It gives you the opportunity to reflect and respond to any revelation the Holy Spirit may have shown you. When I've rushed from a moment I felt God speak, into the next thing, I tend to miss nuggets. Your time in prayer at the end, even if brief, will give you a moment to allow what was revealed to soak in. I've found praying to God out loud and verbalizing what I heard him say has helped me to remember the Bible more.

Reading the Bible has become one of my favorite things to do. Reading my Bible is a very intimate moment with God, Jesus, and the Holy Spirit, where I often feel they're speaking directly to me. Sometimes, they are speaking to a fear I'm wrestling with. Other times, they are speaking encouragement over me. And sometimes, they're helping to correct me. Regardless of what they are saying to me, the theme is the same: love.

Over the years, I've learned that reading your Bible is fun. I have often looked at my time in the Word as a rigid act with God and, in the process, placed Him in a box that read, "no fun here." I thought about having a section titled, "Read with fun in mind." It can be easy to look at the Bible as a rule book for you—you shouldn't do this or that—but the Bible is a book of freedom and life. It's okay to have fun while reading God's Word.

His book is a book of love. He ultimately loves us deeper than any of us could begin to imagine. Have fun discovering God's character, seeing areas you need to correct, learning what it is to live righteously, discovering your Savior's love for you, and seeing how much you've grown. The Bible is this beautiful gift our Father has given us. God always authentically desired for us to be in communion with Him. When you pick up your Bible, that's exactly what you're doing, communing with the Father. Pick it up, value it, have fun with it, but most importantly, love it.

TAKING OFF THE MASK OF THE WORLD

AUTHENTIC

PART THREE: LIVING AUTHENTICALLY WILL REQUIRE...

The mask has been lifted, the authentic plan of God has been revealed, now what do we do? We are called to live differently as believers but in order to live authentically it will require a few key things to be addressed.

AUTHENTIC

LIVING AUTHENTICALLY WILL REQUIRE...

Knowing What to Take Off and What to Put On

What Not to Wear

I used to love watching the show *What Not To Wear*. I think it was on TLC. Stacy London and Clinton Kelly helped someone who seemingly didn't know how to shop or pick out clothing that fit their body. They'd give them a budget, pick things out, and would suggest tips and tricks for how to shop. In addition, they did their hair and makeup. It was a full transformation. At the end of the show, they'd stand before the people they loved for their big reveal.

Of course, most times, people were blown away. Part of me is curious as to whether any of them slipped back into wearing what they did before and if they just got tired or overwhelmed by so much change. When we live a life submitted to following God, it will always cause us to have to change in some way, specifically the ways of sin. God isn't running a makeover show with us, but He is guiding and teaching. And while the show is fun to watch, I think its title sticks, *What Not To Wear*.

No one has ever said to me, "That jacket of pride? It doesn't fit you and looks horrible on your body. And those loose pants of apathy? They have got to go." Following God's plan for our lives will hinge on our relationship with sin. If we are willing to entertain it and not give it the seriousness that God does in the word, all other areas we will speak about in this section will fall short. We can't entertain an appetite for sin and God.

One of the hardest parts of watching the show *What Not To Wear* was when the two stylists told this person they had to let go of their old clothes. They were going to take them and donate them. They would be gone. Unavoidably each time, the person tended to burst into tears, getting emotional and sad. They'd grown attached to the clothes; they had grown attached to how they felt when they wore them.

This can be true for us too, when we look at sin in our lives. Sin has infiltrated every area of our lives. Sin isn't merely failing to obey the Ten Commandments. Sin is any decision I'm making that goes against the voice of what God has spoken to me or anything I'm desiring or valuing above God. If God told me to lay off sweets and I ate a cookie, I sinned. If God told me to forgive someone and I choose not to, that's a sin. If God asked me to give financially to the church and I didn't, that's a sin. If I watched something on T.V. that was sexual in nature, that's a sin.

I believe Satan has done a great job trying to get us to narrow our eyes on what sin could actually look like. And in the process we have unknowingly been exposed to and engaged with things that have become boundary lines between us and God. They have been inhibiting our effectiveness for the Kingdom. Our stylists are God and Jesus, and there are things they are going to ask us to give up, to let go of forever, regardless of how comfortable we feel in bitterness, frustration, greed, sloth, or lust. He has a whole new wardrobe.

Goal: Taking Off Sin

By now, you've realized our clothes are figurative. I'm using this analogy of clothes to tie to sin we pick up and take with us daily to our jobs, the coffee shop, the store, and our families. Sin impacts how we see the world, ourselves, and it also translates to our hearts.

In the third chapter of Colossians, we see Paul addressing the church of Colossae. Paul went there to address their transformation of the original gospel. While they believed in Jesus, they incorporated pagan traditions and other philosophies into Christ. He was on a mission to correct these false teachings within the church. Before Paul said what to put on, he said what to take off.

> **Put to death, therefore, whatever belongs to your earthly nature: sexual immorality, impurity, lust, evil desires and greed, which is idolatry.** Because of these, the wrath of God is coming. You used to walk in these ways, in the life you once lived. But now **you must also rid yourselves of all such things as these: anger, rage, malice, slander, and filthy language from your lips.** Do not lie to each other, **since you have taken off your old self with its practices and have put on the new self, which is being renewed in knowledge in the image of its Creator.**
> Colossians 3:5-10, NIV, emphasis added

Paul addressed what they have put on, a belt of sexual immorality, a hat of impurity, an earring of lust, a purse of greed, shoes of anger, a few bracelets of rage, a skirt of malice, a top of slander, and some lipstick of filthy language. They were wearing these things, believing they were okay to dabble with it a little here and there. We have to be aware that it is easier to excuse poor behavior, than it is to walk away from it. Paul is aware of their sin, even though they aren't. In their minds they have been doing what they perceived to be right in God's eyes, yet were missing the mark completely. It is easier to read the word of God, than to live it out. Paul is pointing out that before I can tell you what to put on, it's crucial you understand you've been wearing some things that don't fit you.

Where are you entertaining sin in your life right now? Where have your eyes grown dim, to the heart of God? Are there any areas you feel far from God? Sin has a way of distracting and pulling us away from our love, God. Sin is a love issue. Love unifies, sin separates. Love covers, sin exposes. Love heals, sin binds. Love corrects, sin indulges. Turning from sin is as simple as falling more in love with the Lord.

And as we grow to love Him more, we love His people more. Our sin issues are merely a love dilemma. A hangup between what we desire in the flesh and what we desire in the spirit. The antidote to sin is to not stop. Stopping in and of itself without love will not last. The antidote to sin is to love the Lord more. Sin my friends has to be taken off and when it is we are clothed with something far better.

Outcome: Clothed By God

*So in Christ Jesus you are all children of God through faith, for **all of you who were baptized into Christ have clothed yourselves with Christ.***
Galatians 3:26-27, NIV, emphasis added

*Therefore, as God's chosen people, holy and dearly loved, **clothe yourselves with compassion, kindness, humility, gentleness and patience.***
Colossians 3:12, NIV, emphasis added

Here in Galatians, Paul talked to the church in Galatia. Paul found himself trying to bridge the gap between new believers who were Gentiles and the Jewish law. He expressed to the people in the church that they are clothed in Christ through their baptism. If you're reading this and have never been baptized, what's stopping you if you already believe in Jesus Christ? Baptism is mentioned many times in the Bible as a step we are to take that symbolically represents the washing away of sin in our lives. Paul illustrated to us that when they became believers of Jesus Christ, they were to put off their old way of thinking about religion and the law and pick up their new garment, which is righteousness found in Christ. We are to be clothed in Christ and His righteousness.

When we do this we begin to wear: compassion, kindness, humility, gentleness, and patience. Of those five things, does any one part stand out to you? To me, patience stands out. I often struggle to put on patience for myself and, at times, for others. I get frustrated and tense easily when something is rubbing up against my patience. And with two little ones, it's easy to find my patience being tested regularly throughout the day.

The reason I asked you if any stand out is because I believe we can have on pieces of the wardrobe but find ourselves struggling with one particular item. It's like I have the whole wardrobe on—compassion, kindness, humility, gentleness, and patience—but the tag on my shirt that is patience keeps scratching and irritating my back. I'm clothed with patience because Christ is patient, but I notice a little friction. This is an indication I should examine or ask God to give me awareness. Don't assume because you have an irritation that the garments are not on, but maybe instead that the belt is too tight and cutting off your airflow. You can ask God to help you adjust it.

Renewal Requires Repetition

Putting on a new self, one that detests sin, is connected to being renewed in the knowledge and image of our creator, Jesus. Renewal is both instant and takes time. It's instant in that when we give our lives to Christ in a moment of belief, we are washed of our sins. We are forgiven. Instantly. But it takes time when it comes to our mindset because we've created pathways of thinking and living. Our brain likes to do what is easiest, what's most comfortable. So, if I've been living in the sin of lust for twenty years, thinking my mind will instantly change is naive. It takes the repetition of thoughts and patterns to have a different pathway of thinking. Any athlete has to train and repeat reps, whether that's strokes in the pool, pitches of the ball, or tumbling on the mat. Repetition is what teaches their muscles to eventually be able to operate to their fullest capacity.

Clothes shopping used to be one of my favorite things. Picking through the aisles, searching for a few shirts that would look cute with the jeans I already had, or maybe finding a fun flirty dress to wear out with my girlfriends. Times have since changed. I find shopping for clothes to be nerve-racking and frustrating. I don't often want to spend the money on them or find myself back in the rut of thinking I always need to buy clothes to stay on trend.

I've come to not even like how clothes fit me because trying to keep up with changing size charts can make any woman irritated. I have similarly grown increasingly irritated as the world has tried to dress me, throwing me justifications for my sinful actions, justifications for why I should not honor someone, and justifications for choosing my own self-will over others. I've worn those clothes for many years, and I have come to realize they don't fit. Some pieces are too tight, squeezing the breath out of me, and others are far too loose.

I want to only wear the clothes Christ has offered me. I have had them all along, and so have you. But it's been masked with layers of other materials and fabrics. Take it off. All of it. You are dressed in Christ, clothed with compassion, kindness, humility, gentleness, and patience. I'm not sure about you, but I don't want to wear anything He's not picked out for me. Styles will change, but what He has clothed me in is timeless.

AUTHENTIC

LIVING AUTHENTICALLY WILL REQUIRE...

Continual Choice

I came to the realization that the biggest hindrance to freedom is choice. Ironically, this came while I was opening my refrigerator, not to get something to eat but to pack something for my daughter as I was going out to meet a friend for coffee. Choice is something that can be both freeing and imprisoning. Freeing because there's no true pressure to do things and imprisoning because it feels, at times, you don't have the option or power to choose.

God gave us choice, and that's a huge part of our free will. But in today's world, I think many of us don't actually feel we have the freedom to do so. And at times when we are given the option to choose, we waffle back and forth unable to make a decision. My friend, Whitney, told me, "When I have freedom, I don't know what to do with it. So, it feels like any other day because freedom feels so unfamiliar to me."

After she finished speaking, her words rang in my head. The thought that we would look at freedom as unfamiliar and never fully step into it because we treat it as common knowledge, shocks me. And if I'm being honest, I have struggled to step into freedom many times in my life because it felt harder than the opposition I had come to know. Freedom is part of God's authentic plan, and that freedom includes choice.

Goal: Freedom

On August 28th, 1963, Dr. Martin Luther King gave his famous speech, "I Have a Dream" in Washington, D.C. I find the beginning of the speech so relevant to our struggle for freedom of choice today.

> *"Five score years ago, a great American, in whose symbolic shadow we stand today, signed the Emancipation Proclamation. This momentous decree came as a great beacon light of hope to millions of Negro slaves who had been seared in the flames of withering injustice. It came as a joyous daybreak to end the long night of their captivity.*
>
> *But 100 years later, the Negro still is not free. One hundred years later, the life of the Negro is still sadly crippled by the manacles of segregation and the chains of discrimination. One hundred years later, the Negro lives on a lonely island of poverty in the midst of a vast ocean of material prosperity. One hundred years later ... "*[10]

When I read this, it all began to click. Jesus came to set us free, not just when we get to heaven, but now. But, just because He came to set us free, doesn't mean that we are free. We have to choose it, and many of us have not. Our lives are plagued with the entrapments of pressures, worry, and fear that cause us to remain in a mindset of slavery versus claiming the freedom we've been given.

The word "poverty" stands out to me in Martin Luther King's speech. If we don't have a free mindset in making decisions and choices, we have a poverty mindset. We begin to assign to our mighty and majestic God values that are less than His nature. We begin to take our definition of our bondage and assign limitations to a limitless God. Have you stopped letting God be free in your life? It's not just about where you'll allow Him access to, but it's also about if you will give him the freedom to operate as He desires in your life, even if He doesn't fit the mold in which you've so desperately tried to force Him.

If we learn to live free with the Lord, we learn to make free choices. It's hard to make choices out of freedom when I feel bound in my everyday life. Our ability to grasp onto the freedom found in our choices impacts how we not only see the world, but most importantly, how we see our God. And when our eyes see more clearly we are able to see through the smoke of indecision and things become far clearer.

Outcome: Clarity instead of Indecision

Indecision or confusion is one of the enemy's tactics to make us feel stuck. Being stuck leaves us hanging in the balance between what we've always done and what we want to actually do; Stuck believing that regardless of which way we choose, we will inevitably feel like we made a wrong decision. But the Lord wants to remove the smoke.

I think for me, the root of this indecision is not wanting to make a bad or wrong choice. I am worried that I will make a decision out of my flesh more so than the Spirit.

Flesh decisions can stem from a desire not to look poorly in front of a fellow colleague. If we make our choices from a place of sin, we are in that instance in bondage to that sin. Think about it, sin is the very thing that causes us to not be in right relationship with God, so why would Satan not desire for our choices to align with him, causing dissension with our Father? Flesh choices aren't just manifested in pride but can also be attached to jealousy, envy, ignorance, and acceptance, to name a few.

*For, as I have often told you before and now tell you again even with tears, many live as enemies of the cross of Christ. Their destiny is destruction, their god is their stomach, and their glory is in their shame. **Their mind is set on earthly things.***
Philippians 3:18-19, NIV, emphasis added

For of this you can be sure: **No immoral, impure or greedy person—such a person is an idolater—has any inheritance in the kingdom of Christ and of God.**
Ephesians 5:5, NIV, emphasis

We tend to make decisions based on what will cause the least friction or tension in our life, but making free choices may actually create a little disturbance or wake. God's Word says we are not supposed to conform to this world but be transformed by the renewing of . . . what? . . . our minds. Freedom is not a worldly value. Yes, we live in a free country, we have the freedom to vote, and the freedom to carry arms, but in many of our everyday lives, we live enslaved. Enslaved to the need to feel accepted.

Danger: Fighting For Acceptance—It Steals Your Freedom of Choice

Okay, let's talk about the "A" word, acceptance. There is something in all of us that desires to be accepted by our peers, to be seen as valuable, or as significant. But let me pose this question: Does the Bible say we should be seeking acceptance? Acceptance is not a part of God's will for our lives. It doesn't mean that there won't be times you are accepted, but it does mean that acceptance can't be the driving force behind making choices. The desire for acceptance leads to more bondage. Acceptance is a dangerous word.

Acceptance says I want to blend in with the status quo. Acceptance says I value the opinion of people over God's opinion. Acceptance tells me what God spoke to me needs to be altered before I bring it before people, because I may face some backlash. Acceptance says my core value is affirmed by flesh, not divinity. I believe our desire to want to be accepted is actually a level of idolizing something other than God. Could the desire to feel accepted be driving some of the choices you're making? Could a desire for acceptance be part of your mask with the pressure to prove?

Let's do a quick survey. In the past month, how many days did you feel the freedom to choose what your day consisted of? Now, when I say this, I know that if you're a parent, caretaker, or have a job, there are things you have to do. But also, be aware, in each of those situations, you could be making excuses to compensate for poor boundaries and a desire to want to feel accepted.

If we are striving for man's acceptance we will not be able to make decisions from a free place. Because the desired outcome is man's approval, not God himself. Desiring acceptance steals your freedom. It's time to start making free choices. Choices that are centered on the finished work of Jesus on the cross. Choices that are rooted in freedom and not bondage.

AUTHENTIC

LIVING AUTHENTICALLY WILL REQUIRE...

New Goals

What is the last goal you set? And what was your desired outcome? I can think of many financial, spiritual, and career goals our family has set over the years. But the most recent one has been around working out. I really began working out consistently after our first child was born. It was a way to get back some confidence, self-love for my body, and to care for what God has given me. When I first began, my goal was to lose weight. In my head, I needed to get back down to the weight I was when I got pregnant or less.

Every day, I worked out and ate right, and the goal remained the same. Some weeks came with great excitement as pounds fell off, others with great frustration. But the outcome I was desiring was to get back into my pre-pregnancy jeans. For months, I worked out tirelessly, trying to attain "what I used to be." If you're a new mom, let me give you a tip. Embrace the current time in your life. It won't ever come back. Stop trying to rush to be a version of yourself that was before children. We try to run back to the ways that exhausted us, trying to meet demands that no longer fit our maturity or lifestyle, all while trying to meet expectations that were never handed down by our Father.

Things have changed.

A few months ago, I decided to start a new workout program, and the goal was quite different. The goal didn't change because I had lost all the baby weight; the goal changed because I had a change of mind and heart. God will do that to you if you allow Him. My goal this time was to care for my body, have fun, and not stress about the scale. The goal was consistent obedience to working out. The outcome changed as well. Gone are the days of me striving to try and fit back into something, but instead, the outcome is me having a good workout and feeling good about it, even if I only gave it 50% that day.

A changed perspective on goals actually has the ability to alter the whole direction of what God is doing in our lives. Before we go any further I want to make sure to give you a definition for the word goal. Goal is the end toward which effort is directed.[11] So goals should be focused on directing our efforts to Kingdom minded living. And what better place to start, than obedience.

Goal: Obedience

Goals are a way of the world. I can't think of a time, except when I was a kid when there weren't goals. I remember goals in athletics, goals in school and grades, goals with SAT scores, and goals with career choices. Goals are not bad things. They can be great, but it's more a matter of what we fix our focus on.

One of the major goals of our society today is success, which has an outcome of possessions, money, affluence, and comfort. Don't believe me? Turn on your TV, where people are settling and compromising morals to gain what they perceive as success. Our society celebrates athletes, celebrities, and musicians as a marker of what success is.

While writing, there have been moments of checking myself, moments where I've had to ask God and the Holy Spirit to search me and know my heart, exposing the unhealthy places that didn't align with His Word. I've come to realize the goal for all of us, in any situation, is the same. The goal in everything we do is OBEDIENCE. This should bring some relief, but likely, it doesn't. Why doesn't it? Partially because obedience doesn't consult me. Obedience will cause us to sacrifice things, laying down things we value. The goal in writing this book was obedience, not success. I write because God told me to. I write on these topics because God told me to. The goal is to complete what was asked and to do it promptly, without hesitation. At times, obedience will try and halt you, slow you, so you don't hurt yourself or others along the way. It will tell you that you're not ready for the platform or success you perceive you can handle

Think about Abraham and Sarah, they wanted what they wanted. Their goal was a child. It wasn't happening in their timing, so they skipped obedience and created the result they wanted. The only problem was, they did it the wrong way, yet God still blessed them with Isaac. The outcome was Ishmael being cast away because he was considered a threat to the possible lineage of Isaac.

Shadrach, Meshach, and Abednego had a goal of being obedient to God first. So, when they weren't willing to bow down to Nebuchadnezzar's statue and worship him, they were thrown into a fire, like a hot fire. I can't imagine how scary that would have been at that moment. But their consequence didn't persuade their goal. The outcome of their obedience was their lives being saved in the fire, and then the lives of the people, including Nebuchadnezzar, turning to God.

King David had a goal to have sex with a woman that he was lusting over while she was in a bath. The outcome was he both inflicted death and experienced it. He killed Uriah, Bathsheba's husband, and then experienced the death of his child with her not long after.

Mary had a goal of being obedient to God, carrying Jesus even if others rejected her. The outcome was her bringing forth and being the mother of Jesus Christ, the Messiah and Savior of the world.

Satan had and still has a goal of turning people away from the gospel and power of Jesus to him and his Satanic ways. The outcome, as we already know, will end in him being thrown into the lake of fire, along with the beast and other false prophets. They will be tormented continually, day and night for eternity.

You can read over and over again in your Bible the plans of man and the outcomes of God or about the plans and outcomes of God lived through man. We must be aware and careful not to set our goal as low as the world; to merely think that everything is about more cars, money, power, followers, exposure, and fame. We were actually never created for any of those things. That was never God's authentic plan. This is why people find themselves depressed when they actually achieve or experience them. Because, like Solomon said, "'Meaningless! Meaningless!' says the Teacher. 'Utterly meaningless! Everything is meaningless.' What do people gain from all their labors at which they toil under the sun? Generations come and generations go, but the earth remains forever" Ecclesiastes 1:2-4, NIV.

Outcome: Knowing More About God

Now, you may be thinking, if I start with the right goal, I should be fine to land at the right outcome. But the truth is, starting with the right heart and goal doesn't guarantee you won't end up off track with your outcome. I realized this not long ago as I was working on something, and had all the right motives with the goal, but ended up in a ditch when it came to the outcome. I had managed to end up in a hole because the outcome became about my self-reliance. It started centered on Christ, and it ended with me having to produce and do a bunch of things to make it happen. The outcome we should always be looking for is to know more about God.

If we've been put here to live authentically, and our authenticity is based on how well we are living in relation to how God made us, knowing more about Him is key. We often think the outcome is about if something was successful. How many people showed up to the event? How much did we fundraise? How many people liked what I posted? Did I buy a bigger house than last time or a nicer car? Did we take a more expensive vacation than last year? There are so many other questions I would venture to put in here.

My friend told me one time, "Depression lives in the past, and anxiety in the future." Are we partially anxious because we are trying to create outcomes in the future that align with our plans instead of God's plans? It does take energy to go against the will of God, to go against His ways, His plans. Philippians tells us, "Do not be anxious about anything, but in every situation, by prayer and petition, with thanksgiving, present your requests to God. And the peace of God, which transcends all understanding, will guard your hearts and your minds in Christ Jesus" (Philippians 4:6-7, NIV). When is the last time, in the midst of your anxiety, that you stopped to pray, to focus on God? To fix your mind on the now? If we don't focus our outcomes on God, we will live a life where we pick up and drop anxiety regularly, because we are trying to live in the future or manipulate it.

Challenger

I was watching a documentary on the space shuttle "Challenger" that exploded on January 28, 1986, just after takeoff. The documentary interviewed family members and reflected on what went wrong on that day. The goal of the Challenger was to get into space. NASA, at the time, was feeling pressure to get in the air.

"What it found was a stunning lack of communication—almost as if officials had been playing a game of broken telephone, with the result that incomplete and misleading information reached NASA's top echelons. And among that ill-translated information were concerns about the O-rings. The issue was completely absent from all the flight-readiness documents.

That wasn't the end of it. During a teleconference some 12 hours before launch, Thiokol engineers told NASA management about their concerns over the O-rings. Overnight temperatures were set to drop to 20 degrees, which raised additional ice concerns. An early morning inspection confirmed that the launch structure was covered in foot-long icicles, and no one knew what would happen if they broke off and became sharp debris. The risks were deemed appropriate for launch. The Commission ultimately flagged the root cause of the accident as 'a serious flaw in the decision-making process leading up to the launch.' Seven lives could have been saved if concerns about the O-rings had reached the right people, or if Thiokol had worried more about safety than satisfying its major customer."[12]

The goal of NASA was, of course, important—getting to space. But the real tragedy happened when they became hyper-focused on the outcome of getting to space, so much so that they compromised their protocol. Success to them was the spaceship being in space, not protecting the seven lives that were on board.

What would it have looked like if they had canceled the whole thing as it was streaming into living rooms or as people watched live? I think it would have looked like a failure to NASA. So, in a desire to not look like they didn't have it all together or like there was an issue, they decided to go along with the launch. I think we have many people in churches, jobs, homes, and life that are just going along with the flow so as to not interrupt the streaming for those who are looking in on their lives.

But which matters more, where you actually end up or where your neighbor thinks you are?

Danger: Silencing God

When we try to control the narrative, the goals, and the outcomes of our lives, we limit the power and ability of God and the Holy Spirit to move in our lives. Let me be clear to explain that the power of God is not removed; He is always moving, always speaking. He doesn't require our obedience to speak. He's omnipotent. But in silencing God, turning Him down a notch or two, we lose the ability to receive from God because we've blocked His frequency.

For example, when you are riding in the car and choose to silence the radio or that podcast you're listening to by muting it, it doesn't stop the communication on the other side. In fact, you just miss part of what's being discussed. When we silence God, we aren't actually removing His ability but ours. Just look at Jesus. He never chose his goals over God's goals. His life was a reflection of obedience. Think about it. Jesus is referred to in Mark 6 as a carpenter, implying that at some point, He worked with His father.

"Carpenters at that time would have created mainly farm tools (like carts, plows, winnowing forks, and yokes) and things that were part of houses (doors, frames, posts, and beams). They also would have made furniture and kitchen utensils. But carpenters could not go to a lumber yard and buy smooth, pre-cut lumber. They would have had to cut down trees and use tools to chop, chip, and smooth the wood. They would have used axes, hammers, saws, planes, and chisels (1 Samuel 13:20; 1 Kings 6:7; Judges 4:21; Isaiah 10:15; 44:13). Carpentry work was physically challenging, causing the carpenter's body to be sturdy and muscular."[13]

Now, if Jesus was put here to share the gospel and to die for our sins, why did he spend years doing physical labor and building things that didn't point to His preaching to come? Why wasn't He practicing His speaking or maybe even plotting how to find a good disciple? Jesus was being obedient to the goal God had for Him and, at that moment, it was to be a child and learn from Joseph. It wasn't to plan for His ministry fifteen years ahead. Jesus wasn't moaning to God saying, "Why, God, am I having to do all these laborious things? I mean I'm not even going to need these skills. Also, I thought I was sent here to preach the gospel."

I imagine Jesus learned things about God as He cut down trees and struggled. I imagine God was teaching Him to pray while He was amongst the trees, that God was giving Him a glimpse of the physical toll that ministry would have on Him in the years to come. One could argue that the physical labor of carpentry that Jesus lived reflected the struggle ahead: the stubbornness of people's hearts. As difficult as it was to chop down and chip away at the lumber, it would be even harder to chip away at people's old points of view on religion and the Messiah. The heart can be far harder to break down than wood.

If Jesus would have said, "Let's just get to it God—no carpentry or waiting." What would the outcome have been? Not what we read about for sure. It would have been centered on Jesus' desires and would have silenced God's speaking and leading. We silence God when we push forward or drive to attain something He has not assigned to us.

We silence God in our pushing. When He said to rest, when we strive, when He said to sit, when we clinch, when He said to release, when we control, when He said to trust. When outcomes become something we try to manipulate and control instead of desiring to know God more, we will always fall short of the full measure of His presence and His blessing.

God created us to be intertwined with Him, Jesus, and the Holy Spirit. That was His authentic plan, to be connected, not just in some parts of our lives, but in all parts. God desires to be the leading area, not just in our finances, but in our goals. We are living in a very goal-driven society. More than community and relationships, people strive for numbers and benchmarks. Can I just say these things are killing us? They're partially killing us because they're causing us to set selfish and self-serving goals centered on our own greed. And it's also killing us because it's driving a wedge between God and us.

The beauty of setting a new goal is an opportunity to let go of what was and to start fresh. Our minds are waiting to be transformed by new ways of thinking. Our hearts are waiting to beat differently because of our obedience. Our spirit is longing to know the Lord more because we desire new outcomes. And God is desiring that we would want to hear His voice more loudly than ever. I'm ready to direct my effort and energies into Kingdom-minded living. Are you?

AUTHENTIC

LIVING AUTHENTICALLY WILL REQUIRE...

An Acceptance of the Mantle

Living a life of authenticity with God will eventually bring you to a point, if not points, where He asks you to accept the mantle He's placed on you. A mantle is something God has given you responsibility to fullfill here on this Earth. When I first started following Christ, I remember sitting at a Christian Leadership conference in Atlanta and having the Holy Spirit say He was going to call me into ministry.

At the time, I was still wrestling greatly with sin. I had friendships that made me desire to run back to my bad behaviors. I didn't deserve to be used by God. But I remember that moment so vividly. The Holy Spirit was calling me out, telling me things as I'd known them to be were about to change, that I'd have to walk away and let the things I loved in the past be burned to ashes and become a servant to Him and His will, not my own.

I remember when I got baptized at New Season Church in Hiram, Georgia, I had a similar moment. I felt the sin that had entrapped me fall off of me as I came out of the water. It was a tangible feeling of peace and release. God calls each of us to carry a mantle, for His name's sake. To carry with honor and with weight a gift or gifts He's given to us, to help others know Him more. Just because He has a mantle, an assignment for your lives, doesn't mean you will accept it.

Goal: Accept the Mantle

I wonder how many followers of Jesus and God have dropped their mantles? They have decided, "I'll just leave it here because it seems too heavy to carry where I'm going." Or maybe, even the thought that the mantle won't let you go where you desire to go has entered your mind, so you just dropped it. Now, this is wild to me. How we chase after status, things, and influence, yet God gives us a mantle from His Kingdom, and we choose, "Nah, it's not worth carrying." As a reminder, when I'm referring to mantle, I'm merely saying God has given you responsibility on this Earth to fulfill something. God didn't put us here to graduate school, get a job, buy a house, start a family, work, and then retire at a good age. While we experience those things and God is in them, they aren't our sole purpose and not even our main purpose. Our main purpose is to fulfill a responsibility God specifically gave to you and me.

In the book of 1 Kings, we see a mantle exchange between Elijah and Elisha. Elijah, who was a prophet, was told that he needed to anoint three men, one of which would be his successor, Elisha. Elijah went to anoint Elisha: "So Elijah went from there and found Elisha, son of Shaphat. **He was plowing with twelve yoke of oxen, and he himself was driving the twelfth pair. Elijah went up to him and threw his cloak around him.** Elisha then left his oxen and ran after Elijah. 'Let me kiss my father and mother goodbye,' he said, 'and then I will come with you'" (1 Kings 19:19-20, NIV, emphasis added).

If God chooses to place the mantle on you, He's equipped you with not only the abilities you need but the patience, endurance, and courage to prevail in times of difficulty. God's given you the Holy Spirit and prayer to intercede when you're unsure. God doesn't make mistakes when He bestows mantles. A mantle is significant to God, even if it isn't to us. For someone to trust another with something of significance is huge. Realize that mantles aren't cheap. Mantles are glorious, they are beautiful, and they are life-giving. We treat God-given responsibility and gifts, at times, casually or even as expendable. I want you to imagine for a moment that you buy your best friend or family member an extremely expensive car as an appreciation for them. You find out months later that the car was scratched up, dirty, or, better yet, they sold it to a dealership for money. What's your response?

Likely, you're upset. You gave something to someone you loved as an act of love. You wanted them to see how much you appreciate them, how much you believed in them, and you wanted them to be able to use it. Now, imagine how God feels every time He asks you to do something for Him because a mantle isn't just found in huge things but in the small moments. When I stop and give money to a homeless person, I'm living out the mantle I've been given—to love others and help those in need. A mantle could be a job that God wants you to leave and a whole different industry He wants you to go into. Would you be willing to lay down what you've known, what has made you successful in a season, to follow the voice and plans of God? Even if you don't have a guarantee?

Outcome: Leave What You Know

Let's look back at verses 19 and 20 again, "So Elijah went from there and found Elisha son of Shaphat. He was plowing with twelve yoke of oxen, and he himself was driving the twelfth pair. Elijah went up to him and threw his cloak around him. **Elisha then left his oxen and ran after Elijah. "Let me kiss my father and mother goodbye," he said, "and then I will come with you."**

Just think about how awkward this would be. It's hot, you're sweaty, and here comes a man you've not met before, and he just throws his cloak over you? Elisha immediately responds the opposite of how many of us would. He responds with urgency to follow Elijah. I believe many of us would want to weigh the positive returns versus the negative returns. We'd maybe even say, "I need to pray about this." There would likely be hesitancy from most of us to suddenly drop what we know, what we're good at, and what we make a great living off of and go without question. Real talk, could you do it, no questions asked?

If we weren't arguing with God about if He really spoke, we'd likely be going through the questions we have. We all have an inner critic. Sometimes he or she is louder than we expect. The dialogue may look something like this.

Me: "But God, I don't think I can follow you, I've not got it all together. I mean, do you really want to use me in this area? Don't you know there's someone out there that speaks better, that's more organized, or even more skilled? I'm not the most confident person either. I struggle, at times, to feel worthy or even just trust what I hear. You know I love you and this is a huge honor, but I'm not sure I'm the one you want."

Have you ever been here? Disqualifying yourself, putting yourself down, and making it all about you? This inner self-talk is me-focused, not God-focused. Leaving what you know will likely have moments where you find yourself focused on yourself. To be honest, the enemy wants us to choose ourselves so we walk away afraid of what God could use us to do. He wants us to choose our will over God's will. He loves to turn it into a "me, me, me" conversation.

Leaving what you know doesn't always look like moving across the country. It looks like leaving friendships behind that God says are toxic or not beneficial, it looks like leaving behind and dealing with old mindsets, like leaving behind the pursuit of your own desires over God's, it looks like giving up a hobby because it's got the potential to become an idol. There are many ways God can call you to leave something behind that you've known. It's not exclusive to one of a few areas. When He asks you to leave something behind, it's because He has something else for you. He knows it has the potential to cause you to stumble or leave your mantle altogether.

Elisha left behind his fields and lifestyle and inherited the gift of prophecy and the ability to minister to people on behalf of God. Abraham left the land he knew and inherited a son and descendants as numerous as the stars. James and John left fishing and inherited the teachings of Jesus. Ruth left behind her family to go be with Naomi and inherited a husband, Boaz. Jesus left his life on the cross so we could inherit eternal life with him and the Father. We have to leave things behind to have room for the things God desires to give.

Danger: Chasing the American Dream Not the God Dream

Elisha went from a man of influence to a servant. By all standards today, this is counter-cultural. People are working so hard to live the "American Dream" that being a servant isn't on the agenda. May I just say, the "American Dream" and the "God Dream" are drastically different. If this is the first time you've heard this, sorry to burst your bubble.

The American Dream: The American Dream is the belief that anyone, regardless of where they were born or what class they were born into, can attain their own version of success in a society in which upward mobility is possible for everyone. The American Dream is believed to be achieved through sacrifice, risk-taking, and hard work, rather than by chance.[14]

While I'm not equipped to define God's dream fully, I can pull from His Words to formulate what I believe He would define it as.

The God Dream: The God Dream is to believe and trust in the Lord God above all else, to follow His ways by first seeking His Kingdom. It involves giving one's life to Jesus and then turning to live a life of righteousness. It includes giving to those in need without judgment, turning and repenting for one's sin regularly, sharing the gospel, loving others as yourself, and living a life of humility. It is to give up one's will, desires, and own life for God.

I pulled this definition from these passages of scripture: Proverbs 3:5-6, Proverbs 31:8-9, Matthew 6:33-34, Mark 16:15, Philippians 2:1-4, Ephesians 4:1-6, Luke 10:27. I'd encourage you to look up each one and see what God reveals to you. If we are chasing the American Dream about us and our mobility, we won't be able to chase the God dream about Him and His name made known.

> **Then he set out to follow Elijah and became his servant.**
> 1 Kings 19:21, NIV, emphasis added

Elisha willingly became a servant. He didn't argue with Elijah, but he followed him, served him, and learned from him. Sometimes we think we know it all, even as adults. Unfortunately, that habit isn't always outgrown with time. But as we think we know it all, we can find ourselves believing we don't need to be servants. Someone who carries a mantle without service is not in alignment with God. Jesus himself did not come to be served but to serve (Mark 10:41-45).

Here's a quick check. Do you find yourself thinking you're too good to do something at work or you're past that point, so you dish it off on another? Do you think you can't learn from someone new to your company because you have tenure? Do you think that another parent can't teach you something because they have a three-year-old and your youngest is sixteen? Do you think you're above taking the trash out at work or cleaning up the bathrooms? There are many more questions I could pose, but I wonder: are you more concerned with your American image that you've decided to no longer be a servant to God's own image?

Imperfect Rock on Which to Build a Church

Part of accepting the mantle of God in your life is also realizing you're imperfect. But that doesn't disqualify you. So many of us, myself included, have had moments of feeling like we aren't "good enough" to step into the call God has on our life. We just need to clean up a little more. Learn a little more. Know Jesus a little more. Even writing this, there are some days I've thought I'm not enough. God chose someone else, someone who is a writer. Alex Seeley, Lysa TerKeurst, Jennie Allen. But He chose me. He chose me because He knew I'd be obedient. He chose me because He knew I'd ask every day, "Holy Spirit, what do you want to write? Guide me. Show me. I will follow your lead." And He's choosing you. We may be imperfect, but we are still usable.

God has had me in process, teaching me over the past year. Removing things from me. If you had met Ashley seven years ago, you would have seen a woman who was career driven. I worked until I was exhausted, and there was always more to be done. I found value in my title and my status at my job.

I now find myself, as I'm writing, seeing that God is using something from a past season that was unhealthy, as a call for this season. I shared how I was a workaholic, driven, exhausted, and found identity in what I did. That has been what the Lord has been undoing over the past two and a half years of my life. He's been undoing the bogus measurement scales I have imposed on my life. He's shown me that the only one I should find my identity in is Him, that exhaustion is not a biblical principle but an earthly one, and that being driven is often also linked to sin, such as pride, and can lead to a continual celebration of bad living.

The very call of me writing this book is imperfect. It was birthed out of mistakes and misaligned value systems, but God has a way of using the imperfect masterfully. The very man Jesus built his church on was doing his best, just like you and me.

Peter was fishing when he met Jesus and left everything to follow Him. There was no formal seminary class or school he'd attended, and yet, this is the man that Jesus said, "And I tell you that you are Peter, and on this rock I will build my church, and the gates of Hades will not overcome it" (Matthew 16:18, NIV).

Jesus didn't nominate Himself, he chose Peter. Peter was imperfect. I mean, he's known for being impulsive and for denying Jesus. Before denying him three times, he tells Jesus he won't deny him. "Peter replied, 'Even if all fall away on account of you, I never will'" (Matthew 26:33, NIV). He also managed to fall asleep after Jesus took him and the two sons of Zebedee to pray with him in the Garden of Gethsemane. He fell asleep multiple times after Jesus had asked him to pray, just like we likely would. Don't pretend like you don't get tired after a big meal and a long day.

I have always found it interesting how quickly one can point out the things that disqualify them or make them unworthy of something. Odds are you could give me pages full of reasons as to why you can't be used by God due to your imperfections. Yet, when we look at others, we believe they have the power to be used regardless of their imperfections. Somehow, their imperfections aren't as intrusive as ours.

God uses imperfect people. Peter wasn't trying to fall asleep at Gethsemane, but he did. He made a human error. He wasn't intentionally trying to deny Jesus, he just let fear creep in. He wasn't trying to lie to Jesus; his actual maturity and faith weren't nearly where he thought it was. Each of those moments served as a marker for Peter. But they didn't stop him from being used.

When God calls you to carry your mantle, it is for the edification of the body, not your own individual platform. You may have made yourself the center if you have decided not to step into the call God asked of you because you, "aren't mature enough," "aren't old enough," "aren't healed enough," "aren't brave enough," "aren't well versed in scripture," "aren't sure if He actually spoke to you," or "aren't _____." If God asks you to do it, it's merely your responsibility to be obedient to it. Where we get wrapped up is in trying to produce something versus living for today's bread alone and allowing God to produce whatever outcome He desires.

God wants you to pick up your mantle, not because of what you can get from it, but so that His name will be glorified. His name, His Word. It's simple. We all have different mantles but the mission is the same, share Jesus' love and make Him known.

There will be moments in your life when God is trying to give you a mantle. Ultimately, we have the free choice to take it or leave it. He will not force our hand. When those moments come, I want to remind you what a gift it is to be chosen by God for a purpose. Our world runs after purpose and identity, but it's founded, most often in self-preference, not God. Accepting His mantle means that you are choosing a God dream. You will have to leave behind the things that you've allowed to name you in the past and disqualify you. You'll be asked to continually humble yourself as his servant. You know, when I think about the words "servant of Christ," it makes me emotional. It reminds me He thinks we're worthy of what we don't think we are and that He trusts us even though we don't trust ourselves. He has chosen you and me to represent Christ to the world, authentically. And we will have to carry our mantles to do so.

AUTHENTIC

LIVING AUTHENTICALLY WILL REQUIRE...

Acknowledging that the Plans Have Changed

I'm a planner by nature. There's just something about lists and being able to check things off. Also, being a parent, I know it's overly necessary to make a list because I have a mom brain. It's a real thing; kids cloud your memory. I made a joke the other day that I believe that mom brain is focused on keeping your kids alive and a few other bare necessities. Nonetheless, I love structure and lists.

Just as I'm great at making grocery lists, honey-do lists, and checklists for chores around the house, I have a tendency to make a list of what needs to be accomplished in my life. You have a list—maybe yours includes getting married by a certain age, or having your first kid by a specific time, maybe even when you want to buy that first home, or get that promotion at work. I have yet to meet a person who doesn't have at least a small list. And whether your list can fit on a post-it note or takes up a spiral ring binder, I've come to realize that as God changes you, your list and plans do too.

Goal: Erase Your List

Have you made room for God to erase your list and write a new one? I know even as I write this, I'm a bit convicted. I have the tendency to allow God room to write the list, but I still want editing access to go in and make some edits as I see fit. Living authentically according to His plan means I have to trust Him, and I don't have access to edit. I have to realize the access to edit what God desires to do in my life may also cause me to miss out on opportunities and blessings only He can give through His plans.

But let's be honest, following God's plan is hard. No one tells you when you give your life to Christ, you will enter into a lifetime of learning to submit. That submission is part of the process, and obedience will be asked of you and me. For many of us, I think we don't like submission because we regard our plan as the better plan, and we struggle to trust God. Our struggle with trusting Him has nothing to do with His character but everything to do with us. Somehow, we think we have the better master plan and that God certainly couldn't have something greater planned.

The reality is, His list always leads to greater holiness and wholeness. Our lists often lead to more earthly desires like money, possessions, and meaningless gains.

Over the years, my personal plan has included staying at my job and starting my own business. But, God's plan for me was to leave my job and work on my character instead as a stay-at-home mom, while writing this book. Writing this has been both liberating and also confusing. It's been liberating because I realize now that healing is a process, and I do believe that, at times, writing about your healing can free and expose things. It's almost like you get to see your growth from a different angle.

But this has also been confusing. Why? Because it wasn't on my list. My list didn't say to sit down and write because I'm not a writer. God, don't you know I'm not an author? The things that have gone through my head during this process have been mostly playing the same tune: I'm not good enough or smart enough for this. This was not on my list. Working at my old job for many years more, that was on the list. Then once that shifted, starting an interior design business was on my list. And yet, here I sit at my kitchen island, typing and writing with anticipation of a breakthrough for women, believing I'm not worthy, but that this has always been on His list.

I believe if we are to live authentically, we have to leave room for Him to write a different list. Can I dare say we are unwilling to let God rewrite our list because we are afraid of what He may ask us to do that feels like we are unworthy, not smart enough, or good enough? Or are we afraid of what He will ask us to give up? I promise you that allowing God to take hold of the list will inevitably lead to change. And there are three areas that will be necessary to let go of, if we are going to let our Lord lead our list.

Outcome: Three Things Get Left Behind With Your Plans

When I read Mark 1:16-20, it shocks me every time with the depths of Simon, Andrew, James, and John. These were average men supporting families. Yet, here they are in a brief but powerful interaction that changed everything for these four men.

*As Jesus walked beside the Sea of Galilee, he saw Simon and his brother Andrew casting a net into the lake, for they were fishermen. "Come, follow me," Jesus said, "and I will send you out to fish for people." At **once they left their nets and followed him.** When he had gone a little farther, he saw James son of Zebedee and his brother John **in a boat, preparing their nets.** Without delay he called them, and **they left their father Zebedee** in the boat with the hired men and followed him.*
Mark 1:16-20, NIV, emphasis added

They left everything they planned, what their family had likely planned, and followed Jesus. There was no delay, they followed at once. They left three things: their nets, boats, and father. When we release our plans and lists, I think we also have to leave behind at least three things.

To follow Jesus, they left behind their logic, desires, and ideals. When it comes to releasing or laying down your plans, you have to let go of things happening logically. Logic is a comforter to us. It's something we lean on because it creates certainty. Not following the plans you have for your life will naturally cause uncertainty, but it's not scary. It may be, at first, but you will grow to learn to live in uncertainty and to know God is working in it. The world teaches logic and doing what makes sense. God teaches trust, and sometimes trust doesn't make sense, so we can't reason away God. Faith is also built upon trusting God. The reason we can even believe in heaven or hell is that we trust God's Word is truthful. There is no way to see it logically before us, but that's where faith enters. "Now faith is confidence in what we hope for and assurance about what we do not see" (Hebrews 11:1, NIV). Your desire for certainty and logic will have to be released with your plans.

All throughout life, I believe, God is continually asking us: Do you desire me and my ways more than you and your ways?

I'm having to remind myself I desire Him more than the salvation of family members. I believe He can soften their hearts so they can receive the gospel, but I desire Him more than what He can do for me. I want His proximity more than His provision. I can't begin to imagine what these four men had to surrender, likely living a life of comfort or safety and certainty for their wives and families. They likely didn't desire to die for their faith and be persecuted for it, but they surrendered their desires to pick up His.

I saved the best for last . . . you have to give up your ideals to follow God's plan. Ideal is defined as a conception of something in its perfection.[15] You and I think our plans are perfect. In our eyes, they make sense. This isn't a new thing, it's happened for thousands of years. People believe they know what's best for them and how to best achieve it. I just want you to read the definition again: "Ideal is defined as a conception of something in its perfection."

I only know of one person who's ever fit this definition, and it surely isn't me. Jesus is our ideal, Jesus is our ideal, Jesus is our ideal. Therefore, He's the one we should look to when it comes to plans for our life. According to scripture, Jesus' only plan was to do the will of His Father. Doing the will of God means we have to be in relationship with Him regularly. Jesus, our ideal, lived that for us to see.

You and I will never be perfect; if we could, there would be no need for Jesus. Yet, here we find ourselves thinking we have the ideal plans for our lives. Look around: people everywhere are dying trying to attain "the ideal" in physical form, in bank accounts, in their jobs, as parents, as spouses, and the list goes on. People are putting themselves in places of anxiety, depression, and stress, all for perfection. And the funny thing is, most people aren't happy, even when they achieve the very things they were trying to gain. Nothing apart from God is sustainable. God's plans will always require us to lean on Him and Jesus. We will not be able to lean on our logic, desires, or ideals. If we don't learn how to not lean on these areas, we are in danger of allowing our emotions to lead us.

Danger: Emotions Leading the List

When I left my job and became a stay-at-home mom, I realized getting rid of social media was not only needed but also that social media was not beneficial to where I was going. God had me in a season of working on my character, refining my identity, and learning to live authentically. It would be very irresponsible of me to be trying to change and say "yes" to His ways while dabbling in the pool of "like me." God doesn't remove things to harm or hurt us. He removes things to heal us, to show us what we really need to deal with, to show us just how strong we are, and to show us how much He loves us. Jonah is someone who comes to mind when I think about not desiring to submit to God's plans based on emotions.

Jonah's anger all starts when he is told by God to go to, what he sees as, sinful people and give them the opportunity to repent. He, instead, decided to run from God. He ended up on a boat and was thrown off after it experienced turbulent seas due to Jonah's lack of obedience. Jonah remained for three days and three nights in the belly of a big fish until he was vomited out. Eventually Jonah decided to do as God commanded and went to Nineveh.

We can gather that it wasn't on Jonah's list to preach the news of repentance to the Ninivites. Jonah allowed his anger, which we repeatedly see in the four chapters, play a role in both His perspective of people and his decisions for himself. Emotions aren't a bad thing, God gave them to us, but when we begin to override the word of God with our emotions, we need to be aware that it is dangerous. Emotions are indicators but not guides. They point us toward further exploration and prayer with God, not actual truth. There have been moments I've felt emotions that would have led to me doing some very dangerous things that were not in God's will. The emotion felt trustworthy, but it wasn't.

What God was asking Jonah to give up wasn't an actual item but an emotion that was leading him to sin—anger. On the surface, Jonah's desire to not bring the news of repentance to the people looked valid; his emotions seemed to be a good guide. What he wasn't bringing into the equation was mercy and the peoples hearts to repent. Allowing God to rewrite your list and plans may mean that what He asks you to give up is a root sin you run to: judgment, lies, envy, and deception, to name a few. Have you made any decisions lately, merely out of emotion? Do you lean more on your emotions than God's will to make decisions? Do you think you have any sins lead by your emotions you need to repent for?

Our plans and our lists go hand in hand. One simply grasps the other. They become one another's supporting characters. You don't have to live a life constantly making new lists, never satisfied, never happy, overworked, over-stressed, and panicked. There's a better way, friend. You can choose to give the planning to God. I can't promise you that you won't, at times, feel these emotions, you're still very much in a fallen world, and you and I still very much are at war with sin. Giving God authority with the plans in our lives and timelines doesn't erase the effects of sin.

When you release your plans to God, don't expect to not be a bit entangled. You've been operating in the driver seat for a while; it's going to take some time to clear yourself of old habits. It's time for us to stop planning, not because we don't care where our life is headed, but because we know the One who can turn our fishing for fleeting moments of accomplishment into an eternal harvest. I assure you that giving God access to your list will not return void. How do I know, you may ask?

"For my thoughts are not your thoughts, neither are your ways my ways," declares the Lord.

"As the heavens are higher than the earth, so are my ways higher than your ways and my thoughts than your thoughts."
Isaiah 55:8-9, NIV

AUTHENTIC

LIVING AUTHENTICALLY WILL REQUIRE...

Bravery

Bravery is a word I don't use often. I have heard the word a few times in relation to others, but it is a word I desire to be. To me, it embodies this balance between trust and faith. I want you to think of someone that you regard as brave and list out why.

One person that comes to mind is my friend, Raquel. Raquel and her husband, Douglas, are brave to me because I've seen them move many times in their marriage and, as a family, to follow what God has asked them to do. They've shared stories about moving to different states, leaving everything, and starting again. It's this continual place of non-attachment to things of this world and attachment to God's will for their life.

I think we can overcomplicate what it means to be brave. Some might think, to be brave, you have to be a firefighter, police officer, or person in the armed forces. And while I honor and respect those positions and believe they require bravery, I believe the bravery God desires from us, is rooted in both faith and trust in Him alone.

The story of Joshua leading the people to the Promised Land is a story of bravery to me. It doesn't defy our logical understanding of bravery, but, I believe, it embodies God. To me, the Bible comes alive when we understand not just the context but the steps that each act of obedience took. I believe we live in a culture that wants to arrive without adhering to the steps needed along the process. Before Joshua and the Israelites entered that land, there were a number of things that had to take place. And I'm willing to bet there are some things that God wants us to experience or go through in order to walk bravely into who He made us to be.

Step One: Crossing Over

For forty years, the Israelites wandered in the desert. After the death of Moses, as Joshua was about to fulfill what God asked him to, I imagine the people were expecting something new but had an old mindset. I imagine they wanted to leave the desert and get to a land that was lush but didn't want to deal with the discomfort of change. But, being brave or courageous requires that we cross over to something new or uncomfortable.

Even as I write, I'm crossing over from allowing this world to define my standards to allowing God's Word to. What that practically looks like is separating myself from hurry, stress, and full schedules to spend time alone with the Father. It looks like letting the Holy Spirit transform the way I see myself and what's been spoken over me. It looks like learning to not be afraid to wage war with the Devil and that I am as broken and in need of Jesus as anyone I'm praying for.
I believe bravery isn't just exhibited in big feats but is a daily choice to live a life in obedience and in alignment with who God says you are. Notice I didn't say who you think you are. Many of us are living with bogus definitions of identity that have left us trapped and limited to only being the most minimal version of ourselves. I don't want to be that, I want to believe that if God's Word says to be bold and courageous, I'm making decisions that reflect that.

As the Israelites crossed over the Jordan, they had nothing but faith as to who God was and what He'd do on their behalf. They trusted Joshua and believed God spoke to him. So they crossed on faith and trust. One of the things I'm realizing is that living a life bravely will cause you to face areas where you don't actually have faith or trust. The thing about crossing the Jordan is you are acknowledging that there is no real way back to where you were. It is also important to mention that what and where he may ask you to cross may look impossible or more difficult than usual.

Now the Jordan is at flood stage all during harvest. Yet as soon as the priests who carried the ark reached the Jordan and their feet touched the water's edge, the water from upstream stopped flowing. It piled up in a heap a great distance away, at a town called Adam in the vicinity of Zarethan, while the water flowing down to the Sea of the Arabah (that is, the Dead Sea) was completely cut off. So the people crossed over opposite Jericho.
Joshua 3:15-16, NIV

The Jordan was at flood season, meaning, the moment God wanted them to cross was the most dangerous and impossible-seeming time. I mean, "Come on, God! We already have to cross this huge river, leave behind what we know, and now you want us to cross at the peak point of flooding?" God can ask you to trust Him and move in faith at times that don't make sense on paper, to people, or during a time littered with transition. But bravery requires that we don't always use logic; sometimes, we just need to trust and obey.

Step Two: Mark the Moment

"Each of you is to take up a stone on his shoulder, according to the number of the tribes of the Israelites, to serve as a sign among you. In the future, when your children ask you, 'What do these stones mean?' tell them that the flow of the Jordan was cut off before the ark of the covenant of the Lord. When it crossed the Jordan, the waters of the Jordan were cut off. These stones are to be a memorial to the people of Israel forever."

So the Israelites did as Joshua commanded them. They took twelve

stones from the middle of the Jordan, according to the number of the tribes of the Israelites, as the Lord had told Joshua; and they carried them over with them to their camp, where they put them down. Joshua set up the twelve stones that had been in the middle of the Jordan at the spot where the priests who carried the ark of the covenant had stood. And they are there to this day.
Joshua 4:5-9, NIV

After obeying and crossing over the Jordan, God commands them to mark what just happened. The marking of the moment wasn't for them but for the generations to come. God wanted the stones to serve as a reminder to their children of what He had done. When you are going through seasons where you're stepping into new levels of bravery or courage, mark them. Not as placeholders to remember what you did but what He alone did.

How you never thought you could forgive that person, but you did, through the power of God. How you never thought you'd be able to pay those medical bills off, but you were able to because of someone's generosity. How you never thought you'd be able to have those kids because the doctors told you that you couldn't, yet you have four kids now that you carried in your womb because God gets the final word.

You may be thinking, "Ashley, how are those moments of bravery?" Bravery is faith and trust in God, and if you forgive someone you have been angry with for years, you said I trust God to be my protector and release the power in this situation. It's brave to accept help when in need; it's an act of humility, not pride. It's brave to believe God can give you the very thing all reports are saying "no" to, and it's brave to speak life over those babies while you're carrying them instead of living in fear.

We can think very much about the future. Planning then trying to align things in the now to achieve what we want later. It's almost like this weird hamster wheel. But to me, what's even odder is that we plan for our children when it comes to money for college but are not nearly as diligent in investing for their future faith and trust in God. Our children have to make their own decision to follow Jesus, to live a life defined by their Father's Word, and to live a life of faith and trust. But we get to be the examples or models for them to look at and maybe even one day emulate.

We all have traits or habits that we've inherited. Think about it. I know for me, some of my similar family traits or habits include: liking to work outside or get my hands dirty, working out, eating healthy, being direct, hardworking, and desiring to have a clean home. I also have been told my sister and I laugh similarly and have similar smiles. Where did I pick up all these features, one may ask? I can't think of a particular time or place when I decided to imitate these habits or traits. They just happened after prolonged exposure meshed with my personal experience. Your children, nieces, nephews, cousins, parents, grandparents, friends, church members, co-workers, bosses, and anyone else I forgot are watching you. Some will emulate what you do. The beauty about all of it is it should serve as a means to point back to what your God has brought you through.

Step Three: Some Things Will Have to be Circumcised

There's no easing into this one . . . to live a life of bravery, there will be things that have to be cut away and removed completely. There is no other way to get the outcome of living with courage. Circumcision was first mentioned in the Bible with Abraham as he circumcised all the males. Circumcision symbolized the cutting off of the old life and accepting a new life with God. You can't desire to be brave and yet allow yourself to purposely return to old mindsets. I understand there are times you can't always control the random thought that pops into your mind or random discouragement that seems to come knocking at your door, but you can choose to turn from it, pray, and move forward. The Bible tells us to submit ourselves to God and resist the enemy and he will flee. The old way of thinking may have been to sit in your thoughts, beat yourself up, and shame yourself. There is a new way, a new covenant that God has for you.

We live in a society that wants "more, more, more." We add more to the calendar, college experience, and our homes. And while we are master adders, we suck at removing things, let alone allowing God to remove things. What's the last thing God asked you to remove?

For me, it was my planning. Don't worry, I'm okay. For all my Enneagram Ones out there, you likely cringed. God asked me to come to Him daily and to not fill my schedule. Since I gave Him my planning, I've been more rested, relaxed, and most importantly, in communion with Him. It's funny, we can try and give so much to others, but we miss what he wants us to do now. God was removing distractions so I could sit with Him, be obedient to Him, and be reminded of my heart's desire to love Him. Removal can expose our unhealthy tendencies, but it can also remind us of what's most important.

I don't believe God's primary goal in removing things is to hurt us, but to draw us closer. That is all he cares about, being closer to us, his sons and daughters. He cares about us living in relationship with him.

But while we are offended to see our unhealthy habits, sin, or failures, God already saw them all. He saw His perfect, blameless Son Jesus hanging on the cross with our sin. And He couldn't ignore it. Think about it, if Jesus was God in human form, then God Himself had to look at what was a part of Him, rejected, beaten down, abused, and mistreated. What would ever make you think that if you feel lonely or weird, God Himself didn't experience the same things, through Jesus, His Son? A parent cares more for their child than themselves; they long to protect and care for them. God felt that way with Jesus and with us. Part of living bravely means that things have to be removed, but take heart, He's doing it for your release.

Step Four: A Different Pace

I'm a clean freak. I love a clean home. To me, it just feels more inviting and relaxing. So ever since I got married, my husband knows that I like to clean the house once a week. It varies in scale, based on how I feel that week, if we have guests coming, or if we are trying to do a seasonal clean. Every now and again, I will ask my husband, Jason, to jump in and help. Now, if you're a clean freak like me, you know that you like things done a certain way. In your head, there is a road to efficiently cleaning. After asking my husband to help one week, I, of course, asked him how long it would take. His response was one I wasn't expecting. He said, "I'm not as fast as you, so it will take me a little longer." My first thought was, *Yep, I am fast. So fast.*

Now, months removed from that conversation when I asked him to help, I find myself cleaning slowly. That's right, the pace of my cleaning is now a turtle's pace compared to before. I realized that while going fast seemed great, efficient, and effective, going fast puts stress on me, takes the joy out of the process, and I may have missed a few things. In an effort to accomplish something at record speed, I compromised my health. Shocking, I know. And when I say health, that can mean peace in place of stress, or our mental state. My clean freak nature is gradually fading as I learn to live at a different pace.

Joshua followed what God asked, even when it didn't make sense or wasn't what was done in the past. In those spaces of faith and trust, Joshua revealed his bravery. I think we have an image that bravery is all about us. It's driven by us, dependent on us, and operated by us. But true bravery isn't possible apart from believing in God's Word and living a life in alignment with it.

> *Now the gates of Jericho were securely barred because of the Israelites. No one went out and no one came in. Then the Lord said to Joshua, "See, I have delivered Jericho into your hands, along with its king and its fighting men. March around the city once with all the armed men. Do this for six days. Have seven priests carry trumpets of rams' horns in front of the ark. On the seventh day, march around the city seven times, with the priests blowing the trumpets. When you hear them sound a long blast on the trumpets, have the whole army give a loud shout; then the wall of the city will collapse and the army will go up, everyone straight in.*
> Joshua 6:1-5, NIV

God tells these men to march around a securely fortified Jericho, and to do this for seven days straight. If I had been one of those men, there are a thousand things I would be thinking. *Why don't we just fight them by breaking through the gate? Won't they see us marching around the city for many days? Why wouldn't they then attack us? This isn't how we've done things in the past. Do you think Joshua heard correctly?*

The Israelite people followed God's command. He adjusted the pace. When God adjusts the pace, it doesn't mean that you're less effective or less gifted. We can think that if God slows something down, it means we are not living rightly or we've done something wrong. But that's not true, God can shift pace for what's to come, to produce something in you that is impossible apart from a different stride.

Isn't it funny how He had them walk? The pace was not frantic, but leisurely. I do think it's important to note that just because He adjusts the pace, it doesn't mean that we should not move with intention. We can think that because God slowed the pace of a season, we can grow complacent or lazy. We are to be good stewards of all that God's given. Even though the pace had slowed for Israel, the pace of the walk still had intention. It makes me think of men and women in the military; how when they walk in groups, it has order and intention. Be careful to not grow distracted during these times. It's easy to do. An adjusted pace requires discipline that speed doesn't.

We see Israel do just as God commands, and on the seventh day, the walls of Jericho fall. The men proceeded to invade the city and kill all living things with the exception of Rahab, the prostitute, and all who were with her in her house, for she had helped the Israelite spies escape when they had spied out the land. Joshua and the Israelites would go on to conquer thirty-one kings and their cities. Their bravery was apparent throughout the land. I wonder if you had the chance to ask Joshua or one of the men who were a part of the army of the Lord if they thought they were brave, what they'd say. I believe they'd sit us down and tell us about the ways they trusted the Lord and how He moved on their behalf; how they had faith and trusted in situations that seemed wild, but to them, it was normal.

Living a life of authentic bravery is rarely seen in this world. This bravery is based on people who are continually choosing to trust God, day in and day out. These people exhibit bravery that says:

I don't have to mimic the pace of this world, because my God is the God of all time.

If God wants to remove something from my life, that only means he wants to give me something greater in return.

I will choose to remember God's faithfulness regularly and share it with my kids.

I will pick up and move my life, all because of a word from God. I'm more concerned with trust and faith than security and complacency.

It's time we start walking and living a life of bravery, unhindered by the agendas of others but focused on the mission of the Father. Living bravely will require work; it will require a changed set of priorities and behaviors, but bravery isn't accomplished in you alone. Quit living timid and scared, you have a brave Savior and God who are waiting for you to trust Them.

TAKING OFF THE MASK OF THE WORLD

AUTHENTIC

CONCLUSION

My hope for you as you complete this book is that you would know the Lord's voice a little better, that you will have set down something you were never intended to carry, and that you are walking away more aware of how to live an authentic life. Following the voice of God won't always look like starting a company or walking away from your job, but it can look like many small daily decisions to say "yes" to what matters most.

Yes to peace and not pressure to prove.

Yes to your family instead of another meeting.

Yes to God's word.

Yes to sharing the gospel with that friend or co-worker.

Yes to listening to the Holy Spirit.

Yes to accepting the mantle God has placed on your life.

Yes to walking in confidence.

Yes to God rewriting your life plans.

It's time to live free friend. It has always been a part of God's authentic plan.

BIBLIOGRAPHY

1. "Mask." Merriam-Webster.com Dictionary, Merriam-Webster, https://www.merriam-webster.com/dictionary/mask. Accessed 5 Mar. 2023.

2. "Subjugate." Merriam-Webster.com Dictionary, Merriam-Webster, https://www.merriam-webster.com/dictionary/subjugate. Accessed 7 Mar. 2023.

3. "Authentic." Merriam-Webster.com Dictionary, Merriam-Webster, https://www.merriam-webster.com/dictionary/authentic. Accessed 5 Mar. 2023.

4. "Authentic." Merriam-Webster.com Dictionary, Merriam-Webster, https://www.merriam-webster.com/dictionary/authentic. Accessed 5 Mar. 2023.

5. Merriam-Webster.com, s.v. "Water down," accessed November 25, 2022, https://www.merriam webster.com/.

6. Topical bible: Storeroom.

7. Honda, Mineko. "Luke 5:39-What Are the Old Wine and the New Wine Mentioned Here?" Core. Accessed November 25, 2022. chrome extension://oemmndcbldboiebfnladdacbdfmadadm/https://core.ac.uk/download/pdf/229750848.pdf.

8. Thesaurus.Plus, s.v. "Storeroom and Storehouse Are Synonyms," accessed November 25, 2022, https://thesaurus.plus/related/storeroom/storehouse.

9. What the Bible says about new wine as God's holy spirit. Ac-

cessed December 14, 2022. https://www.bibletools.org/index.cfm/fuseaction/topical.show/RTD/cgg/ID/19230/New-Wine-as-Gods-Holy Spirit.htm.

10. King, Martin Luther, Jr. "I Have a Dream," Talk of the Nation, NPR, Jan 14, 2022.

11. "Goal." Merriam-Webster.com Dictionary, Merriam-Webster, https://www.merriam-webster.com/dictionary/goal. Accessed 15 Mar. 2023.

12. Teitel, Amy. "What Caused the Challenger Disaster?" History Stories, A&E Television Networks, LLC, January 28, 2022. Accessed November 25, 2022. https://www.history.com/news/how-the-challenger-disaster-changed-nasa.

13. Rodgers, Justin, Miller, Butt, and Staff, "Carpentry in the Bible."

14. Adam, "American Dream."

15. Dictionary.com, s.v. "Ideal," accessed November 27, 2022, https://www.dictionary.com.

AUTHENTIC

www.ingramcontent.com/pod-product-compliance
Lightning Source LLC
Chambersburg PA
CBHW030334100526
44592CB00010B/696